GUSTAV MAHLER

This memoir, by another of the twentieth century's great conductors, portrays not only Mahler the composer but also the conductor and the man. Bruno Walter first met Mahler in 1894 while working in Hamburg and was to be profoundly influenced by his complex musical personality. In 1901, at Mahler's invitation, Walter went to Vienna to become his assistant and director of the Vienna Court Opera. He was Mahler's closest colleague and enjoyed an intimate musical relationship with his troubled mentor. Mahler played to him the Third Symphony on the piano and gave him full authority to change elements in the orchestration of his symphonies should the accoustics of any particular hall necessitate it. Walter worked closely with the soloists for the première of Mahler's Eighth Symphony in 1910, and, after the composer's death, conducted the first performances of *Das Lied von der Erde* (1911) and the Ninth Symphony (1912).

This monograph remains an indispensable document in the cultural and intellectual history of a vanished epoch.

BRUNO WALTER

Bruno Walter was born in 1876 in Berlin into what he described as a 'modest Jewish family'. Possessing exceptional musical talent, he entered the Stern Conservatory in Berlin when he was only nine years old. Inspired at the age of thirteen by Claus von Bülow, he decided to become a conductor.

An admirer of the artistic ideals of Walter von Stolzing of *Die Meistersinger*, he changed his name from Schlesinger to Walter at the outset of his career. In 1901, Mahler invited Walter to Vienna to become his assistant and director of the Vienna Court Opera, which he remained until 1913. He was undoubtedly Mahler's closest associate and collaborator.

Bruno Walter followed a distinguished career and enhanced many of the greatest opera houses and orchestras in Europe and the United States, where his performances of Mozart, Beethoven, Schubert, Schumann, Brahms, Mahler, Bruckner, Wagner and Strauss in particular were universally acclaimed. It is a tragedy that anti-Semitism and the rise of the Nazis were to force one of Germany's greatest musicians to flee his homeland – first to France and then to America where he died in 1962.

BRUNO WALTER

Gustav Mahler

Translated from the German and supervised
by LOTTE WALTER LINDT
With an Introduction by MICHAEL TANNER

Frau Max
Gacium – 1995
Cincinnati

Ω
QUARTET ENCOUNTERS

Quartet Books

Published in Great Britain
by Quartet Books Limited 1990
A member of the Namara Group
27/29 Goodge Street, London W1P 1FD

A catalogue record for this title is available from the
British Library

Printed and bound in Great Britain by
BPCC Hazell Books
Aylesbury, Bucks, England
Member of BPCC Ltd.

CONTENTS

INTRODUCTION

At first glance this small book is nothing more than a contribution
to the genre of unqualified hagiography, now defunct except for
obituaries in *The Times* and the annual newsletters of educational
institutions. Bruno Walter, great conductor and ardent disciple of
Mahler, celebrates in the unctuous idiom of his adopted home,
Vienna, the artistic and human grandeur of the man who inspired
his career and honoured him with his friendship. The chief
shortcoming of this mode is that it tends to turn everyone into the
same person: the only variables are the times and places, the
specific vocation, the great names. Otherwise the material is
identical: the hero had a difficult life, but rose to all its challenges
and vanquished all the enemies, apart from the one that led to the
writing of the memoir or obituary. He was, to the unsympathetic
outsider, irascible, even cruel; demanding and ungrateful; petulant
and temperamental. But the writer, granted the rare privilege of
intimacy and confidences, was able to see how the tantrums were
an inevitable outcome of the Faustian striving for perfection; that
the rage was directed more by the genius at his own shortcomings
than towards the external world; that at the behest of his exalted
calling he was bound to behave in ways that would shock ordinary
people.

This particular specimen carries these features of the genre to
the verge of self-parody. But in doing so, it also manifests another
characteristic of the species to a startling degree: the self-
glamorization of the writer as he ostensibly abases his own
personality before that of the genius of whom he writes. For there
would be no point in his contribution unless it presumed to have
insights that were denied to less perceptive witnesses of the

genius's stormy pilgrimage through life. Hagiography always has a reflexive dimension, but in Walter this becomes, one feels at crucial points, the main point of the enterprise. He tells, for instance, of an incident which took place when he was still very early in his career.

> Once, when I was conducting *Aida*, the chorus behind the scenes came in about ten measures too soon, probably because the chorus master was expecting a cut often made at that point. I quickly speeded up the orchestra; then, all of a sudden, the chorus stopped, and I had another 'rescue' on my hands! It appeared that, at the critical moment, Mahler had dashed from his box and appeared behind the scenes to silence the chorus and give the entry signal himself; he had not counted on my taking in the situation quite so quickly. I tell this story simply as characteristic both of his impetuosity, and of how entirely co-operative he could be.

Oh no you don't, one feels less than an abandoned cynic in rejoining.

That is only a crudely obvious instance of what Bruno Walter, the Prussian who assimilated to Vienna so completely that many people have thought him the most typical conductor of that city, practised throughout his memoir. But without it, too much would strike one as unbearably bland. Walter himself is usually considered, in contrast to Mahler, Toscanini and Klemperer, the great tyrants of the podium, as the man who demonstrated how it is possible to achieve marvellous artistic results by cajolery and charm. But there is more than one kind of ruthlessness, and Walter's interpretations of the great composers have a demonic element which his self-propaganda has often led listeners to deny or ignore. He remains, in his finest performances of Mahler himself, his master's greatest interpreter. To achieve as complete a realization of the first movement of Mahler's Ninth Symphony as he does in that cataclysmic performance given in Vienna in February 1938 he must have had both a phenomenal control over the orchestra and a vision of anguish and terror to match Mahler's own. The extraordinarily cultivated image of gentleness and smiling humility which he presented to the public is merely a further contribution to the self-portrait that emerges in counterpoint to the Michelangelesque ferocity which he sketches Mahler as possessed by throughout this seemingly saccharine memoir.

But even if, reading this kind of thing now, one is likely to experience it as a period-piece, or with occasional fits of nausea, it does contain some fascinating *aperçus* about Mahler's personality, more about his music, and occasionally one about such matters as the relationship between the work of art and its interpreter. Writing about Mahler's first two symphonies Walter points out, what is obvious to any listener, the influence of Beethoven, pervasively, and of Bruckner from time to time. But then, more strikingly, he adds, 'There are echoes of Berlioz, too, in the daring use of bizarre and grotesque means for the purpose of reaching the utmost keenness of expression; he perhaps learned more from the great French genius than from anyone else,' and immediately one recognizes an insight that deserves prolonged pondering. Because Mahler's musical idiom is so obviously post-Wagnerian, with strong elements of Schubert and Bruckner, it is natural to think of his distinctiveness, as evidenced by startling juxtapositions, ironies and climactic banalities, as being without ancestry. The sheer idea of learning from Berlioz is itself somewhat weird. But as soon as Walter has advanced it, it seems so clear that one wonders how it could have been overlooked.

The answer to that may lie a few pages further on in the memoir, when Walter tells us that, 'Between these two periods [that of the first four symphonies, and that of the Fifth to the Seventh], [Mahler] was absorbed in Bach; *The Art of the Fugue* had a profound influence on his counterpoint.' It is typical of the rather slapdash manner of the memoir (but it was written in 1938, at a time when Walter's whole life was in upheaval as a result of the *Anschluss*) that he leaves the reader to bring together two such disparate influences as Berlioz and Bach. Of all the great composers, none is so free of counterpoint as Berlioz, who employed it in *La Damnation de Faust* only in order to mock it, and not very adroitly. The methods that Berlioz used to evoke nightmare, disintegration and the soul in ceaseless turmoil were angular, irregular melody and phantasmagoric orchestration. When he is successful, the result is a powerful communication of a sensibility not so much divided as distracted; and so the fragmentation that he registers is a linear one.

Mahler is concerned with a more complex kind of psychic disorder, in which different strands of the personality are in conflict. Hence his study of Bach, creatively put to purposes which Bach would have been wholly bemused by. In Bach's world, counterpoint always moves towards, and can be felt to be moving towards, order and thus harmony. In Mahler, counterpoint is required to articulate his sense of the radical incompatibility of the elements of our experience. In his greatest and most typical works it is used to give voice to the chaos in the soul, and his heroic battles result not in the peaceful resolution of the warring elements, but in the triumph of one over the rest, so that his textures become thinner, evoking both the elimination of disorder and a final tenuous thread of being, as he moves towards a peace which is indistinguishable from resignation, exhaustion, a cessation of conflict which can only be achieved by surcease. Final contentment is the same as oblivion. Only unconscious Nature, forever renewing itself, can console us with a valid image of immortality. Hence the Ninth Symphony and *Das Lied von der Erde* are greater because more honest works than the Eighth Symphony, which makes a colossal bid to demonstrate the truth of something much more like the Christian hope, but betrays itself by the very strenuousness of its assertions.

Walter, the incarnation of the will towards universal concili-ation, can see that Mahler is too realistic to allow that this can be achieved but is also intent on claiming that that is precisely what Mahler *did* achieve. This failure to cope with the Dionysiac pessimism of his subject leads to the fruitful confusions of the chapter on 'The Composer', where he is clearly at his happiest in dealing with the early works, which from the perspective I have been sketching are evidently immature. When it comes to the great central trilogy of purely orchestral symphonies, Walter is so perplexed by the intransigence of Mahler's terrifying vision of life that he is forced into simultaneously denying it and sketching what it is. About the Sixth and Seventh Symphonies he writes, 'Both of the latter are as unmetaphysical as music can be, in them the composer is concerned to expand the symphonic idea.' He immediately proceeds:

> However, the Sixth is bleakly pessimistic; it reeks of the bitter taste of the cup of life. In contrast with the Fifth, it says 'No', above all in its last movement, where something resembling the inexorable strife of 'all against all' is translated into music. 'Existence is a burden; death is desirable and life hateful', might be its motto.

One wonders what metaphysical music would be if this is wholly unmetaphysical. So after nearly two pages of accurate though elementary exposition of the content of the middle symphonies, Walter returns to saying, 'These three works needed no words to clarify their conceptual ideas ... I cannot discuss them.' With evident relief, he moves on to the last works, and sums up his account of Mahler's creative work by invoking 'beauty. For beauty is immortal.' No problem.

Klemperer, asked in a television interview what was the difference between himself and Walter as interpreters of Mahler, famously replied, 'Walter is a Romantic moralist. I am a Classical immoralist,' and laughed unnervingly. As a characterization of their performances I am not sure it is accurate. As a pithy comment on the difference in their characters, it surely is. And because Walter was a moralist he had to find in Mahler a resolution which allowed mankind the victory which all Mahler's greatest music denies. It isn't clear to me that the character he portrays in this memoir could possibly exist. It is clear that he is not portraying Mahler, either the man or his work, but a figment of the Romantic moralist's imagination. Strangely, there hasn't yet been a biography of Bruno Walter. When there is, this memoir will be an indispensable sourcebook.

Michael Tanner

PREFACE

Republication of this study of Gustav Mahler makes me ask myself whether I still share its point of view and endorse its content. The answer is Yes, I do.

True, I wish I had gone more fully into many matters, notably the marked change in his work from his Fifth Symphony onward. An extensive literature has, however, gone thoroughly into this development of his inner sound-image and the resultant enhancement of his polyphony as well as his technique, and even his whole symphonic style. On these matters my tentative indications have been sufficiently complemented. I do, however, believe that the passage of time has perhaps given me a clearer understanding of a highly individual man and musician, which I would like to put on record.

I have, nevertheless, decided to leave the text as it stands. This is because I am struck, on taking it up again, by the unity of its tone. I do not want to make alterations or additions that might break the continuity of what I wrote under the strong emotion of the twenty-fifth anniversary of Mahler's death – he died on 18 May 1911 – still less because this continuity was itself the product of my intense absorption in his work and character at the time I was writing. Therefore, I have made up my mind to leave the tone, the tempo, and the total impression as they stand, confining any alterations to this preface. Here, I must be retrospective and take into account the fateful influence of world events on the culture of our century.

Gustav Mahler died three years before the outbreak of the First World War. There was peace in the world in which and for which he wrote and performed his symphonies. The passionate, easily aroused Viennese temperament was therefore forced to find its outlet on the battlefield of music and the arts – a battlefield on which the Viennese citizen felt very much at home. A fighting pose and passionate partisanship characterized the Vienna of that time: Mahler's tempestuous nature was highly conducive to loosing storms about his head. The first performance of his Fourth Symphony led, as I recall, to fisticuffs within the precincts of the Musikvereinsaal. Passionate audience-reaction to his daring music, however, was the rule rather than the exception at performances everywhere; fascination grew out of the opposition as well as the enthusiasm that his works evoked. The impression made by his Third Symphony was overwhelming – and for the first time unquestioned – at the performance under Mahler's baton at the Krefeld Festival of the Allgemeiner Deutscher Musikverein in 1902. It established him definitely in the world of contemporary music. In the years that followed, however, performance of his symphonies often led to angry demonstrations and counter-demonstrations. Among his friends, Mahler met all this 'for' and 'against' with the reiterated conviction: 'My time will come.'

My own experience in conducting his works, and, so far as I can judge, that of my colleagues, goes to justify his confidence. Of course, we have not silenced hostility; his musical and emotional excesses still rouse the critics. But each year sees the impact of his symphonies grow. They triumphed even in Vienna, often so recalcitrant. The strident subjectivity and shrill eccentricity that once roused such opposition came to be recognized as marks of originality. Profound seriousness and lofty ecstasy spoke to the heart. Simple, often 'folksy' themes appealed to the Austrian, while sheer power of symphonic form and masterly instrumentation overwhelmed the more deeply musical. For many years now, a Mahler programme has filled the hall. My colleagues and I had the same experience in Germany. Nobody who heard Mahler conduct the first performance of his Eighth Symphony in Munich in July 1910, a year before his death, will ever forget it. It was a high point in his life as composer.

Up to his death in May 1911, he invariably conducted the first performances of his symphonies, though portions of his Second and Third were given by Strauss and Weingartner before the works were heard in their entirety. Two works, however, he did not conduct: *Das Lied von der Erde* and his Ninth Symphony.

Alma Mahler handed the scores to me for final revision before printing. In November 1911, six months after his death, I conducted the first performance of *Das Lied*, in Munich; and, early in 1912, of the Ninth, in Vienna. It was a heavy responsibility to take my great friend's place and introduce his work to the world. Here was the fulfilment of the sense of dedication which, when I first had been shaken by his First Symphony in Hamburg, had made me see my future as one of service to his work.

The rise of the Nazi regime for a time put an end to performances of Mahler, first in Germany, later in Austria. During the Second World War, my own conducting was confined to America. Acclaim for his work, as conducted by me and by my colleagues, rose steadily, despite the obstinate hostility of some influential critics; today, a wide section of American concert-goers has taken him to their hearts.

The war once over, his symphonies gradually made their way into the European repertoire. I ought, incidentally, to mention that in England they were occasionally performed even during the war. I have conducted them in London, Paris, Amsterdam, Edinburgh, Vienna, Salzburg, Munich and elsewhere. It is not easy, looking back over these impressions, to say where Mahler stands in the musical world of today. Audiences are no less enthusiastic than in former times, a section of the press still stands aloof. His work appears, if not often enough, on concert programmes.

The reaction on thought, feeling and behaviour, and the damage to the spirit and content of culture resulting from two world wars and their long aftermath have been so appalling that it is encouraging to find work, characteristic, despite its originality, of a sane period and developed under the influence of the great classics, holding its place even in our disordered world. Look, for example, at the fatal effects of the crisis after the First World War; art, either 'intellectualized' or proliferating into sheer 'entertainment', was given over to sensationalism and the worship of mere technical proficiency in music, to atonality, to the twelve-tone system, to experimentation regardless of content, and all this within a general climate of materialism and utilitarianism, and amid the conflict of contending political ideologies. We were, in fact, faced with a chaos making it an act of faith to believe in the continued life of art or in the music native to the heart of the genuine musician, of which Mahler's work was a late blossoming – I am fully aware of the threat to our civilization inherent in contemporary developments. I am, however, convinced that in Mahler the coexistence of highly 'modern' harmony and polyphony with profound depth of feeling, ranging from human to divine, ensures the survival of his creative work. What makes me certain of this is that his harmony and polyphony, for all their vivid modernity, remain in the realm of tonality.

The nearest approach to his disturbed and disturbing Ego is, perhaps, *Das Lied von der Erde*. It is his most personal work. His idiom is as daunting and as subjective here, and as hard of approach, as in his late symphonies. But what is always daunting in Mahler is the burning spirit, not the experimenting intellect. That spirit is open to anyone who can feel. Here the approach is made easier by the strange quality of the Chinese poems in which, on the threshold of death, he found inspiration for the fateful colour of the songs.

I cannot speak of *Das Lied* without recalling Kathleen Ferrier's unforgettable performance in the three movements for contralto. From the time of the first production, in Munich, I was lucky in my singers. I recall, gratefully, tenors like William Miller, Jacques Urlus, Charles Kullmann, Martin Oehmann, Peter Pears and Julius Patzak, and contraltos like Mme Charles Cahier, Louise Willer, Sigrid Onegin and Kerstin Thorborg. But one of the most significant encounters of my artistic life was that with Kathleen Ferrier. Her performance in *Das Lied* – as in the *Kindertotenlieder* and other of his songs – remains among the deepest and happiest experiences of my musical life. The lovely timbre of her voice moved me, when I first heard it, as hardly any other sound ever has. And she had a soul as well as a voice. That soul knew and resounded the very soul of Mahler's work. I have often thought how much it would have meant to him to hear the profound understanding in her performance. There was something mysterious about this creature, who appeared so limpid, gay, simple and direct. This mystery interpenetrated her singing; she sounded every depth, released every treasure in works she had made her own. Her secret was unity. Everything about her was lovely: her appearance, her soul, her voice, her expression. She expressed intense feeling over the gamut from charm to tragedy, and was, throughout, possessed of a loveliness like an aura revealing the mysterious grace of her nature. Perhaps her early death was part of the mystery that brooded over the life of a great artist. Deep gratitude mingles in my grief for her loss. To Mahler she rendered a permanent service; permanent, happily, in that, thanks to technical progress, it lives on in her recordings.

My faith in Mahler's immortality is strengthened by a realization of the enduring character of the reforms he carried through in the Vienna Opera. Contemporary productions, designed to realize the intentions of the composer by stressing the dramatic significance of the work and of what is taking place on the stage, date back to Mahler's time as general director, of which I speak in the following pages. Even in the precarious world in which we live there is ground for hope when the flame of a potent personality lives on, incandescent in creation and in reproduction.

As I mentioned in my opening words, I am, despite – or perhaps, because of – the distance of time, conscious of closer contact with a man of genius, to whom I owe much in my own life, a man who was, in decisive years, my model, a man whose deep humanity will always remain with me.

Bruno Walter, 1958

RECOLLECTION

FIRST MEETING

MEMORY goes back to my first meeting with Mahler. I was only eighteen. In June 1894 the first performance of his First Symphony, then called the 'Titan', at the Festival of the Allgemeiner Deutscher Musikverein in Weimar, called forth a howl of indignation from the musical press; critics poured the vials of their wrath on a work at once sterile, trivial, and monstrously extravagant. In particular, the 'Funeral March in the Manner of Callot' was dismissed with irate contempt. The excitement with which I devoured the notices comes back vividly; I marvelled at the singular courage of the unknown composer of the March, and ardently desired to know the man responsible for so extravagant a work.

A few months later, I got an introduction to Pollini, recommending me for the post of corépétiteur (coach) at the Hamburg Opera, where this same Gustav Mahler, whose work had so excited me, was chief operatic conductor. As I came out from my first interview with Pollini, there he was, in the office of the theatre; small in stature, pale and thin: the lofty forehead of his long face framed in blue-black hair, and behind glasses, remarkable eyes; lines of sadness and of humour furrowed a countenance across which an astonishing range of expression passed as he spoke to the various people round him. Here was the incarnation of Kreisler, the arresting, alarming, demoniac conductor envisaged by the youthful reader of E. T. A. Hoffmann's fantastic tales. With friendly kindness he inquired into my musical qualifications and capacity; to his apparent satisfaction I replied with a mixture of modesty and self-confidence. He left me bemused and perturbed.

Having grown up in a middle-class environment, I had looked on genius as something that existed in books and scores, in the thrill of the concert hall, the theatre, the art gallery, whereas one's fellows were likely to be commonplace, and real life dull. Now higher spheres seemed to open before me. Mahler, in aspect and gesture, seemed at once genius and demon; suddenly life took on a romantic quality. I can cite no stronger evidence of the electric effect of his personality than the swiftness with which its impact transformed my entire feeling about life and my attitude towards it.

My next memory of him is at a rehearsal of *Hänsel und Gretel*, then going into production at the Hamburg Opera. Never had I encountered so intense a human being; never had I dreamed that a brief, cogent word, a single compelling gesture, backed by absolute clarity of mind and intention, could fill other people with anxious terror and compel them to blind obedience. An inadequate piano-accompanist exasperated him; suddenly—oh, joy!—he saw me standing in the wings, and asked whether I could take the risk of accompanying *prima vista* an opera I did not know. My proud 'Of course!' produced a smile of amusement; a wave of the hand dismissed my unhappy colleague and set me in his place. In the forest scene, the repeated choral echo was poorly done; he turned to me, saying something like: 'I rely on you to know what goes on in a forest; work out the echoes for me!'

This first rehearsal gave me a real impression of his method of working. He led; he commanded; steeped in the spirit of the work, he knew precisely what he wanted to achieve. Brusque and harsh with weakness or inadequacy, he was kind and sympathetic wherever he recognized talent and enthusiasm.

My third recollection is of a meeting as we were coming off the stage. I was about to take my leave when he stopped me, and said: 'Walk a bit of the way with me.' Of our talk I recall only that it began with a remark of his about Humperdinck's work, which he said was 'masterly in execution, but not really a fairy tale'. From the nature of the fairy tale he went on to other topics. It fascinated me to find the same intensity and high intellectual pitch in his talk as in his rehearsing. The violence with which he rebuffed my insufficient remarks—how shyly I made them! His sudden plunge into reflective silence, then the friendly glance with which he picked up a sensible observation; the unexpected twitches of furtive pain across his face; even the curious irregularity of his walk—now he would stamp; now stand stock-still; now rush ahead—all this confirmed and strength-ened the impression of someone demoniac. Indeed, I should hardly have been surprised if, after we had taken leave, he had flown off in the form of a vulture as Lindhorst does under the eyes of the student Anselmus in Hoffmann's *Goldner Topf*.

A fourth picture completes my first impressions. Mahler had bidden me to visit him; as I walked into his workroom my eye was caught by a reproduction, on the wall, of Giorgione's 'Concerto'. Who, I asked myself, was this monk, with his hands on the keys, who seemed to be interrupting his playing to turn and face me? What had he to do with Mahler, whom he so strangely resembled? Then I realized that for a long time I had been unconsciously seeing Mahler in my mind as the reincarnation of the ascetic music-maker in the picture. Actually, there is a family resemblance here, and not to Mahler only. Somehow every genuine musician resembles the monk, if no one else so much as Mahler. Here is a miracle. A genius of the brush, with the prophetic foresight proper to genius, has here created the typical musician; created him, not built him up out of pieces of knowledge. In Giorgione's time, music as we understand it did not exist. Thus the image of a musician was created in advance of music!

The picture gave the point of departure for our talk. Whether we then touched on Giorgione's strange prevision I do not remember, but I do recall our often speaking about it later. I also know that

Mahler's likeness to the pious player enhanced my sense of the mystery prefigured in the fifteenth-century portrait. On this or perhaps on my next visit, I at last worked the conversation round to his creative work, and persuaded him to sit down at the piano. Then everything I was capable of feeling and understanding was fused in one single, tremendous impression; then the tyro in music was given a thrilling insight into the soul of a creative artist. Small wonder that when I began to have a share in the re-creative work of a conductor who could penetrate to the very soul of great works and enrich anyone who worked with him by revealing, through example and precept, their universal significance, my spiritual experience literally went to my head! That I did not lose my head entirely was owing to the boundless devotion and reverence I felt for him. I was ready, without reflection or even looking forward or back, simply to follow him, to feel and to work with him. Since such an attitude was as natural and as congenial to me as were Mahler's music and music-making, I luckily never lost myself in my devotion. Years later, at the cost of grave soul-searching, I had to break away from his influence. But I say today, as I felt then in the very depths of my being, that his influence was a blessing on my whole life.

II

HAMBURG

I SPENT two years in Hamburg. A few weeks after I started work there, Mahler arranged for me to be appointed chorus director. I had thus, both in that capacity and as co-répétiteur, the advantage of co-operating in his productions and becoming directly familiar with his ideas. Soon I was also conducting opera, and when at the close of my first season Otto Lohse went to America, I sloughed off the skins of chorus master and coach to put on the coveted and more shining costume of a 'real' conductor. It was of course understood that I continued to act as coach for Mahler's productions. It was of immense advantage to me to share with the singers the effort to satisfy his demands for the utmost rhythmic accuracy and strict obedience to dynamic and other markings; the more so because I was naturally inclined to overstress the element of feeling in music, the dramatic and poetic aspects in presentation, and the full expression of the spiritual content of a work at the expense of absolute precision; in general, to sacrifice accuracy to vitality. He taught me to pay increasing attention to accuracy and precision in my rehearsing. When, for his *Rheingold*, I was rehearsing Loge or Fricka, I would do my utmost to achieve a combination of lively expressiveness with the rigorous exactness Mahler demanded of singers. My wanderings in the woods of sentimental error would have been long had I not learned from his example and precept that the highest degree of rhythmic accuracy is the best means to attain the highest degree of dramatic expression in Wagner; and, in general, that confining the spiritual within strict musical fetters is a help and not a hindrance to concentrated and powerful emotional utterance.

A constant subject of our conversation was rubato —i.e., the subjection of accuracy in tempo and rhythm to a slowing down or speeding up for the sake of increased emotional expression. Mahler, even in Italian music, where he recognized a certain degree of rubato as a legitimate stylistic element, was against the excessive use of it in which German musicians and singers indulged. He gave, in an unforgettable performance of *Traviata*, the perfect example of a controlled use of rubato, the melodic line being dictated entirely by fire and passion, not by the fancy of singers.

We had many talks about Wagner. Mahler's lifelong considered devotion to Wagner clarified and deepened my obsession with the subject. He was a convinced Wagnerian, and remained one to his death. My most vivid impressions from his Hamburg period remain his *Ring* and *Meistersinger*; later, in Vienna, came a *Tristan* that, both in its total effect and in many details, will live in my ears and heart forever. We also talked endlessly about Wagner's personality; Mahler never wearied of defending him against 'Philistine' reproaches of being ungrateful and not to be trusted, or of angrily demonstrating how the absorption of the genius in his work serves as an explanation of human frailties. The scope of his analysis was, of course, by no means limited to Wagner; it extended to every artistic work on which he was engaged, although never with any notion of laying down the law to a man sixteen years younger than himself. Mahler was, in any case, no educator: he was far too absorbed in himself, his work, his stormy inner life; he paid too little attention to other people or to other things.

Indeed, anything in the nature of that systematic exercise of influence which is the essence of education was remote from a wholly unregulated nature moved by its own impulses. I soon learned that nothing in his life was systematic; it was more like the central cataract of the middle Nile than any even-flowing stream. In efforts to describe his personality, therefore, no epithet occurs so constantly as 'erratic'. Erratic indeed he seemed to me, though there was no sense of any lack of solid ground beneath his feet; he was ready to rush forward again only when the cataract of emotion and thought had subsided into a temporary calm that lasted—until the next impulse foamed up. He hardly ever gave me any conscious teaching, but there is no measure for what I learned in the deeper sense from contact

with a man who, in word and in music, overflowed
with a sheer abundance of vitality. His abrupt im-
pulsiveness perhaps explains the excitement nearly
everybody felt who came near him; especially, of
course, singers and members of the orchestra. He
diffused an atmosphere of high tension. This was
communicated to those with whom he worked, and
induced devout admiration in the best of them. It
produced performances illuminated by the fiery glow
within him which raised the Hamburg Opera to the
top rank in Germany. Of course, there were weaker
spirits, men of second-rate gifts, who were injured
by his absolutism; good will or ill, however, none
could resist his sway.

At this stage, an extreme mobility was the outward sign of his intense vitality. I can see him now,
at an orchestral rehearsal of *Gotterdämmerung*, step-
ping down from the conductor's desk and hurrying
to the trumpets and trombones to examine a particular passage in the funeral music with them, or
borrowing the stool of a double-bass player to get
up on to the stage in order to deliver instructions
that would have taken longer and been more trouble
from the desk—for example, about the gradations of
tone by off-stage chorus or stage-band. While this
went on, the orchestra would wait silently, as
though mesmerized by the spell of the powerful man
who, himself compelled by his inner vision of a
work of art, had to impose the irresistible demands
of this vision on his colleagues. Not once in the two
years I spent with Mahler in Hamburg, or in the six

in Vienna, did I ever see the spell broken. 'The magic worked' from beginning to end; the tense atmosphere that was his element prevailed.

Such concentration inevitably and naturally brings forth its corresponding counterpart: a considerable absent-mindedness with regard to everything that lay outside the circle of immediate interest, and numerous comical situations occurred because of his distraction. One may serve as a characteristic example. One day, in the course of an orchestra rehearsal, the stage director asked him to pause for a few minutes to allow some important scenic rearrangements. After a brief period of impatience, Mahler became lost in thought. The director, having finished his business, tried repeatedly and unsuccessfully to call him back, until, suddenly aware of the silent expectation in the house, he looked vaguely around, knocked on the stand with his baton, and cried: 'Waiter, my bill!' In the laughter that broke out on all sides, he finally joined, heartily. A deep confusion of this kind is the compensation for, and perhaps the condition of, concentration as absolute as his. For such so-called distractions as cards or any other game, he had no use.

As he gradually realized my passionate interest in his creative work, he began to take pleasure in letting me get to know it, on the piano. I can still hear the droll grotesquerie of his singing *Des Antonius von Padua Fischpredigt*, its insolence in *'Um schlimme Kinder artig zu machen'* and *'Selbstgefühl'*, its passion and pain in the *Lieder eines fahrenden Gesellen*. Still, too,

I can feel the heart-searching excitement of at last getting to know the First Symphony through him. His creative work came more and more to be the substance of our intercourse and our conversations.

As I grew to know him, in these talks, and to know the books he read, the poets and philosophers he loved, my original impression of a fantastic, demoniac apparition from the world of E. T. A. Hoffmann was replaced by one more just and comprehensive, but also far more difficult to understand. I shall speak later of the extraordinary spiritual range of a nature full of contradictions; of the dark forces with which he struggled; of the spiritual longing that constituted the central thread in his life and his work. Here it is enough to say that I understood as much—and as little—of his complex inner life as was possible for one so young and inexperienced. What I did understand fed my increasing reverence for the man, as my growing intimacy with his work fed my increasing enthusiasm for the musician.

How could it be otherwise when a man normally incalculable and explosive was invariably kind, helpful, and sympathetic to me? He never assumed the teacher's attitude; there was no question of his regularly listening in when I conducted opera, or of his supervising my work in detail. But he was interested enough in my conducting to sit in on a performance from time to time, and to give me his opinion on it afterwards. Once, when I was conducting *Aïda*, the chorus behind the scenes came in about ten measures too soon, probably because the chorus master was expecting a cut often made at that point. I quickly speeded up the orchestra; then, all of a sudden, the chorus stopped, and I had another 'rescue' on my hands! It appeared that, at the critical moment, Mahler had dashed from his box and appeared behind the scenes to silence the chorus and give them the entry signal himself; he had not counted on my taking in the situation quite so quickly. I tell this story simply as characteristic both of his impetuosity, and of how entirely co-operative he could be.

Particularly precious in my memory are the occasions when we played piano duets, Schubert being our favourite. We had great fun; Mahler, sitting on the right, would play my top notes with his left hand, and leave his own lower line to my right; each of us thus had all the time to read both *primo* and *secondo*, which introduced amusing complications. He used to invent words to go with various marches, singing as he played. He was great at simple nonsense of this kind; in conversation he loved witty sallies, sometimes comic in their irrelevance. Yet all at once his carefree laughter would be clouded over; he would sink into a gloomy silence that one dared not break.

Quite apart from these sufferings, which had their source in the depths of his being, circumstances in his life gave grounds enough for deep depression. In 1895 his younger brother Otto, of whose musical gifts he had had high hopes, shot himself. There were two symphonies in the drawer of his desk, one of which had been performed but once, and only in part, the other having been received with total lack of understanding—nay, with derision. There were a number of songs with orchestra; three books of lieder, which nobody sang; a third symphony was nearly completed.

Moreover, Mahler's relations with Pollini deteriorated, as was but unavoidable in view of their wholly divergent standards and values. This led to an unhappy situation in the theatre. It made Mahler eager to get away from Hamburg, back to his familiar Vienna and its incomparable musical climate. When his doorbell rang, he would cry: 'Here comes my appointment as the God of the Southern Zones!' But the appointment was long in coming, and he felt a mounting need for some satisfying experience, some major artistic achievement to clear his path for him. He decided to produce his Second Symphony in Berlin, with the Berlin Philharmonic and the Stern Gesangverein. The work was performed in its entirety for the first time on December 13, 1895 (the first three movements had already been given earlier that year). For the composer it was a decisive day. Of the work he once wrote: 'You are battered to the ground with clubs and then lifted to the heights on angels' wings.' The effect, after what I recall as a superb performance, was overwhelming. I can still feel the breathless excitement, in the last movement, upon hearing the mysterious cry of the bird after the end of the world in the *Grosser Appell* and the profoundly moving entry of the chorus—

'Arise, yea, arise!' Even then, of course, there were hostility, misunderstanding, belittling, and malice. But the impression of a great and original work and of the power of Mahler's personality was so great that his emergence as a composer dates from this performance.

And yet, everything might have gone wrong. He suffered intermittently from migraines which, like everything of his, were violent in their onset. They paralysed his energies. When an attack took place he could only lie completely motionless. In 1900, just before a concert with the Vienna Philharmonic at the Trocadero in Paris, he actually lay thus immobile for so long that the concert had to open half an hour late, and it taxed him to the utmost to carry it through. On this earlier occasion in Berlin, after great sacrifices he was staking his whole future as a composer on this event: but there he lay, that very afternoon, with one of his worst migraines, incapable of moving or partaking of anything. To this day I can see him, later, on the exceedingly high and far-from-steady podium, pale as death, his superhuman will-power conquering his pain as he conquered performers and audience. For me, a young musician, that day and its victory were of profound significance. I had thought I knew the work, which I had transcribed as both a piano duet and a piano solo. But when I now heard as living sound what I had only known in my own mind and in its piano setting before, I felt with complete certainty that here was a mission for my life. The music itself, its acclaim, and my resolve to devote my life to Mahler's work made me happy.

Meanwhile, I realized that I had gone as far in my work with the Hamburg Theatre as a young man like me could go. There was no room for promotion for me there. Moreover, my relations with Pollini had become difficult. Mahler advised me to look for another post. He had Breslau in mind, where a second conductorship seemed to offer a favourable opportunity. On his recommendation, Dr. Löwe appointed me, and I left Hamburg after two years. My experiences during this time had shown me the direction; to follow it was my solemn resolution.

III

STEINBACH

EARLY in July 1896 I got a letter from Mahler, which, although it has already appeared in his collected letters, seems in place here:

> Steinbach am Attersee
> July 2, 1896

Dear Friend,

I send a brief reply and invite you to come and see us about the 16th, unless, for reasons I don't know, you have made other plans for your holiday. Perhaps my sisters have told you that I haven't been idle; indeed, I hope that a few weeks will see the entire *Third* (Symphony) happily completed. The first sketches are already quite clear and now I am working on the orchestration. I have no doubt that our friends, the critics, appointed or self-appointed, will once again suffer from dizziness, but those who enjoy the pleasant strolls I offer will find them fun. The whole thing is, of course, tainted with my deplorable sense of humour and 'often takes the opportunity to submit to my dreary taste for dreary noise.' The players frequently 'do not pay the least attention to one another, and my entire gloomy and brutal nature is nakedly exposed.' It is well known that I cannot do without trivialities. This time, however, all permissible bounds have been passed. 'One often feels one has got into a pub, or a sty!' Do come soon, and in your armour! If your taste has been purified in Berlin, be prepared to have it ruined! Warmest greetings to you and your family, and Au revoir!

As ever,
G. M.

This cheerful letter proved that the completion of the first movement of his Third Symphony and the prospect of early completion of the entire work, whose other movements dated from 1895, had put him in good spirits. I looked forward eagerly to the weeks I was to spend with him at Steinbach.

I arrived by steamer on a glorious July day; Mahler was there on the jetty to meet me, and despite my protests, insisted on carrying my bag until he was relieved by a porter. As on our way to his house I looked up to the Höllengebirge, whose sheer cliffs made a grim background to the charming landscape, he said: 'You don't need to look—I have composed all this already!'

He went on to speak of the first movement, entitled, in the preliminary draft, 'What the Rocks and Mountains Tell Me'. But I had to curb my impatience to hear the Third. Nothing would induce him to show me or to play a single note of a work that was not completely finished. This was his invariable rule.

At Steinbach, Mahler was unbuttoned as never before. Close to nature, free of the cares of the opera, wholly occupied with his own work and thoughts, he was relaxed: he could and did let the riches within him play over his surroundings.

On the meadow between the lake and the boarding house where he lodged, he had had four walls and a roof set up to make a room. This little ivy-covered 'composer's hut' was furnished with a piano, a table, an armchair, and a sofa. When the door opened, masses of beetles fell on your head. Here he spent the morning undisturbed by noise from the house or the road. He went there about six a.m. At seven breakfast was silently set before him; the opening of the door at midday recalled him to ordinary life. This ought to have happened punctually at twelve; often, however, it was three before the hungry members of the household and the cook's anxiety about her dishes were relieved. Not that he stayed continuously in his hut; he would wander about the fields, and often took long walks up the hills, returning in order to 'bring the harvest into the barn'. On such days he would appear at lunch highly animated, and conversation was lively. He took a child-like delight in good food, and had keen relish for a tasty sweet; he declared that the cook, being an imaginative person, had to surprise him in this line every day for four weeks! One of his favourite jokes was to assert that this excellent dish must be enjoyable to anyone but an ass—and then to ask his guests how they liked it. In the afternoon we went for walks or made music; in the evening we talked or read. Sometimes he would break silence by reading aloud something that had struck him in the book on which he was then engaged. I remember that he could not keep his enjoyment of Cervantes' *Don Quixote* to himself, and especially that he laughed so that he had to stop reading when he came to the attack on the windmills. He laughed uncontrollably over the doings of master and servant, but what moved him most was the idealism and purity of the Don. He said that, much as it amused him, he could never lay the book down without having been deeply stirred.

He took great delight in two kittens, whose play he never tired of watching. When out for a short walk he would put them in his pockets and enjoy their gambols while he paused for a rest; the little creatures were so used to him that he would play a sort of hide-and-seek with them. He had a warm feeling for all living things and felt a loving concern for dogs, cats, birds, and all the creatures of the woods. He watched them with sympathy and understanding; he would reply with an involuntary cry of delight to the song of a bird or the jumps of a squirrel. He told me that he could never forget an occasion in the country when, listening in the night to the long, deep bellowing of the cattle, he had felt a sympathetic pang for the animal's dumb soul.

Summer in Steinbach passed with the restful uneventfulness that his creative work required. Composition had to be done during vacation-time if, as he wanted, he was to return to the city with the score completed in sketch. Definitive instrumentation and final polishing could wait until winter, but his work as musical director was incompatible with musical creation. At last, at the end of the summer, came the day when he could play me the completed Third Symphony. Thanks to our talks, full of the overflow of the creative frenzy of his morning's work, I was familiar with the spiritual atmosphere of the Symphony long before I knew its musical content. Yet it was a musical experience of an un-dreamed-of and shattering kind to hear him play it on the piano. I was literally dumbfounded by the power and novelty of this music, and bowled over by the creative ardour and loftiness of the work as he played it to me. This music made me feel that I recognized him for the first time; his whole being seemed to breathe a mysterious affinity with the forces of nature. I had already guessed at its depths, its elemental quality; now, in the range of his creativity, I felt it directly. Had he been an ordinary 'nature lover', a devotee of gardens and animals, his music would have been more 'civilized'. Here, how-ever, the Dionysiac possession by nature, which I had learned to recognize, sounded through music that expressed the very root of his being. Now I seemed to see him in the round: I saw him as possessed alike by the stark power of the crags and by the tender flowers, as familiar with the dark secrets of the life of the animals in the woods. Notably in the third movement, he brought everything—aloofness and whimsy, cruelty and untamability—to life. I saw him as Pan. At the same time, however—this in the last three movements—I was in contact with the longing of the human spirit to pass beyond its earthly and temporal bonds. Light streamed from him onto his work and from his work onto him.

The lovely summer came to an end. Mahler's mood was clouded by the approach of the Hamburg opera season. He sighed, with renewed longing, for the 'appointment as the God of the Southern Zones'. I parted from him, but I carried the music of the Third with me, and it was a long time before its disturbing presence passed into secure possession.

In the next five years we kept in touch through steady if infrequent correspondence while I was successively at the theatres of Breslau, Pressburg, Riga, and, finally, the Royal Opera in Berlin. The end of my Breslau contract found me with nothing definite in view. I was considering whether the best way of dealing with a possibly useless period was to do my military service, when Mahler, without one moment of deliberation, wrote offering to cover my expenses for the year. Luckily, I did not need to accept his sacrifice—for it would have been one; at the last moment I was offered an engagement in Pressburg. This, to my delight, carried the prospect of frequent visits to Vienna and of seeing him and hearing some of his performances. He, meantime, had achieved his desire; the 'appointment' had come: on May 11, 1897, he appeared for the first time on the conductor's stand at the Vienna Opera. His *Lohengrin* was a 'volcanic' event; in the autumn he was made Musical Director. It was a thrilling experience to see the man I recalled in a series of vivid pictures of relaxed summer holiday on the Attersee now sovereign over the most brilliant of opera houses. What a change from the limited artistic resources of the small theatre in Pressburg—beginners on the stage and a drab public in the auditorium —where I was 'first conductor', to the glories of Vienna, with the Philharmonic Orchestra in the pit, and on the stage, established artists and the fresh talent Mahler was discovering; a festive audience filling the grand house, and at the desk, Mahler! I revelled in performances of, among others, *Dalibor*, *Djamileh*, *Eugene Onegin*, and *The Flying Dutchman*, which he conducted; his shining example saved me from getting used to insufficiency in my own work. Thanks to my visits to Vienna I got fresh artistic impressions and renewed intimacy with Mahler. He took me into the circle of his friends there and gave me the spiritual stimulus I had so sadly missed during my time in Breslau.

For me, two years in remote Riga followed my stint in Pressburg, years during which contact with Mahler was confined to letters. At this time we had a misunderstanding, luckily our only one! In October 1898 he offered me the post of Assistant Conductor in Vienna, dating as from 1900, at the expiration of my contract with Riga; he added that it would suit him if I could be available in the autumn of 1899.

Here was a problem. I wanted to go to Vienna and
to Mahler. He created a horrid moral dilemma for
me by saying that it was important to him to have
me come before 1900 because if he had to go on
working the way he was working, he would be dead
by then. But I was twenty-two; I wanted to try out
my powers and develop my own responsibility as
conductor at a relatively good opera house like that
in Riga: I was afraid of falling under his spell again
at that stage, and—though I have never thought of
this before—of thereby perhaps deflecting the course
of my own natural development. I wrote to him in
this vein. He refused to appreciate my qualms: I had
disappointed him and left him in the lurch. A cool-
ness that hurt me badly sprang up between us. All
the same, I felt I had to stick to my guns. When, in
1900, I was called to the Berlin Opera, I accepted,
of course letting Mahler know and recapitulating
the reasons for my former refusal. He sent a kind
and forgiving reply. It made me hope that unhappy
episode was buried. I went to Berlin, and after a few
months there, received another invitation from him.
This time I had no hesitation or doubt: I arranged
to be released from my Berlin contract at the end of
the year, and in the autumn of 1901, full of hope and
happiness, took my place at the Vienna Opera.

IV

VIENNA

IT is hard to speak in terms of calm reminiscence of Mahler's period at the Vienna Opera; it seems more natural to recall a ten-year festival to which a great musician invited fellow artists and audiences. It was highly fortunate that, for a decade, a musician of genius and a man of potent will, passionately devoted to the theatre, had in his hands the rich resources of a noble institution; fortunate, too, that his activity there came at a time when his own powers were at the full, and in a period of relative political calm which permitted concentration on the arts.

Mahler was at his zenith. The flame of his spirit burned, during those ten years, with ever more brilliant clarity. His energy grew with the reckless demands he made on it; there seemed no limit to a conscious artistic achievement which the enthusiasm of the public confirmed. When I took up my appointment he had been with the Opera four years: nevertheless, each time before he appeared in the orchestra pit, the audience seethed with the high tension that precedes a sensational *première* performance. As, with his quick, firm steps, he approached the desk, the house fell silent. If there was a whisper or a late-comer edging in, Mahler would turn; whereupon a deathly stillness would fall. He began; everything was under his spell. Before the third act there was invariably such a storm of applause as made it hard to get the performance going again.

It was thus throughout the entire period of his directorship. He conquered Vienna with his first appearance on the podium. His dominion over audiences was unbroken to the last. No attacks on Mahler the opera chief or the composer could dislodge Mahler the conductor. His popularity in this city obsessed by music and the theatre was really extraordinary. As he crossed the street, hat in hand, gnawing his lip or chewing his tongue, cabmen would turn to look at him and mutter, in tones of awe: 'Mahler himself!'

To be popular is not necessarily to be beloved. Beloved, a 'darling of Vienna', he was not; for the comfortable he was too uncomfortable. Yet this strangely unobliging, uncompromising, vehement man certainly exercised an intimidating fascination both in public and in private, on the Phaeacian city which Vienna was before the war. He interested the Viennese enormously. All his doings were eagerly discussed. He did away with the claque. He cancelled the cuts in Wagner. He shut out anyone who arrived late for the overture or the first act—a Herculean achievement at that time! Singers were refused leave. Long-established singers were brushed off. His gruff remarks were the talk of the *Kaffee*-

haüser; his caustic repartee was on every lip. He had a marked gift for neat summings-up. It happened that in his presence I told a Tristan to make a change in his attitude and expression when he swallowed the love-potion, so as to convey total loss of self-control and restraint, and to express this in his voice. Mahler interrupted, saying: 'You have got to remember, dear X, that before you drink you are a baritone, afterwards a tenor!' An influential person recommended a new opera, saying that the composer, though of no particular standing, had this time produced something really lovely. Politely, Mahler replied: 'Nothing is impossible, but it is improbable for a horse chestnut to produce an orange!' He told me that he was inclined instinctively to state things in this drastic fashion, and experience had taught him that it was the quickest and surest way of making himself understood. With a grin he added that this practical result was more important, for his purpose, than the complete accuracy of expression inevitably sacrificed for a neat *mot*. His sayings took the public fancy; a journalist who did a Sunday gossip column was perpetually bothering me for characteristic comments or actions of his at rehearsal: anything of the sort interested his readers. I am afraid he was much annoyed by my refusal to talk.

During Mahler's first years his great performances were hailed with enthusiasm and steadily supported by artistic Vienna; I found there an atmosphere of high-pitched give and take. Mahler rejoiced in being able to use the great resources of the Opera to give

a music-loving public great productions of works he
loved; the public responded by coming in festive
mood. True, before I joined him, he had had fearful
rows with the Philharmonic Orchestra about his
changes in the instrumentation of Beethoven's Ninth
and about his performance with the entire string
section of Beethoven's String Quartet in F minor,
but there was hardly a trace of this left when I
arrived. Musical Vienna was in a state of wild enthusiasm about his incomparable *Tales of Hoffmann*—a
perfect model of imaginative recreation, both scenic
and musical. Over this mood of restored amity only
one shadow lay—his casting policy. He brought out
significant young artists and used them in his magnificent performances. Every time a new star rose at
the expense of the old the resultant hard feelings
were not confined to the artists concerned. Mahler's
attempt to build up a fresh generation of singers
disturbed the public also for another, more important reason. By nature an optimist, he had confidence
and interest in everything new. Artistic creation and
scepticism are opposed to each other—he con-
fidently expected each new voice, each fresh talent
to fulfil all his wishes. At auditions he would listen
hopefully rather than critically, eagerly on the look-
out for the happy surprise of discovery. It irked
him to be surrounded by an atmosphere of cool
objectivity. His constant hopes for great new singers
involved a constant presentation of guest artists; this
tended to overload the repertory, and sometimes
carried disappointment; hopes raised at rehearsal

were let down by public performances of leading roles. Then his impulsive nature would swing to vehement rejection. No such experience, however, succeeded in damping his native optimism. Certainly, when one looks back over the period one sees that he had a golden touch in selection; when one looks at what he found, the eagerness of his search is more than justified. No need to cite the names of his artists; they belong forever to the great days of opera in Vienna.

There was some shaking of heads about his tendency to pay less heed to a singer's purely vocal gifts than to his personality. For instance, to give an outstanding example of a rule followed primarily in the casting of minor parts, he gave the role of Kasper in *Der Freischütz* to a baritone personally admirably qualified to fill the dismal role, because no available bass, however excellent his voice, measured up to his conception of this sinister figure. He never hesitated, when it seemed right to him, to put the dramatic viewpoint before the musical.

His repertory, like his choice of novelties and revivals, was a fine balance among care for established works, for the unjustly neglected, and love of the new. The fresh life he breathed into opera of every genre from Gluck and Mozart to Pfitzner and Charpentier reflected the breadth of his outlook. It was enriched by the inclusion of works that had previously failed to find general acceptance, but showed their worth when presented with imaginative mastery such as his: e.g., Boieldieu's *La Dame Blanche*,

Goetz's *The Taming of the Shrew*, and Halévy's *La Juive*.

As Mahler's repertory left no scope for criticism, attacks had to be directed against his serious handling of new problems. What is now seen and accepted as pioneer work on his part was then in its trial phase; it roused excitement and resistance. I am thinking of his and Alfred Roller's productions of *Tristan*, *Fidelio*, *Walküre*, *Don Giovanni*, *Figaro*, *The Magic Flute*, *Iphigenia*—productions marking stages on his way towards solving what he clearly saw as the whole problem of operatic presentation. I mention this here in passing. I shall deal later with his work as director and conductor. Here it is enough to say that while, to the end, he commanded the support of the worthwhile members of the musical public, who admired the manner in which his daring spirit was pressing beyond normal bounds into the heart of problems, and saluted the reckless vehemence of his pursuit of this goal, there were others. The duller and weaker among his collaborators detested his fanaticism and the violence of his personal utterances. And the more conservative element of the press and public was antagonized by his artistic daring. Anything new irked them. They grumbled. They did not realize that the experiments of today were setting the pattern for tomorrow.

If, in the last analysis, hostility was caused by the challenging stature of his achievement—as is the case with anything new that matters—it must be admitted that he himself was often innocently guilty of giving personal offence. The steel in him reacted against the 'softness' of the Vienna of his day; it was really a salute, with standards in reverse. The dynamic man and fascinating conductor overwhelmed resistance from the very beginning. To maintain this position in a world inclined to take things easy demanded unyielding refusal of any sort of concession. But as his pioneering search led him away and up from the level tract of the accustomed, his artistic demands grew even loftier and more complicated.

Moreover, Mahler, with all his kindliness and sensitivity, was in outward behaviour dominating by nature. He had the gift of command, unfamiliar in a Royal and Imperial Opera House highly conscious of its glorious past. The *genius loci* of the splendid and magnificently equipped theatre resembled, before Mahler's advent, the young man of the world in Giorgione's 'Concerto' rather than the earnest, exalted monk. It was the latter spirit that Mahler brought in, and he was determined to place his stamp on an institution previously characterized by the brilliance of its singers, the sensuous charm of its music-making, and the richness of its décor. Something new and exciting was injected into the sensuous culture of the city by the approach and demands inherent in the profound sincerity of his whole personality, in his spiritual attitude towards his art, and in his relation to the operatic masterpieces.

In his first year as director, he had an audience with the Emperor Franz Josef, who declared proudly

that 'Mahler has succeeded in making himself master
of the House'. Mahler was determined to maintain
this mastery in order to achieve his artistic aims.
He succeeded. But his sights were constantly raised,
therefore his demands grew more exacting and his
methods more severe. Artists of genuine gifts and
sincere intentions, however, never encountered the
sharpness of his edge; he had patience with their
failings and showed his appreciation both artistically
and in personal contacts. For instance, a highly
gifted singer whom he liked used always to make the
same mistake at a certain point in a Mozart opera.
During a performance of this work smoke appeared
on the stage as a result of a short circuit. The audience showed signs of disturbance. Panic was prevented by Mahler's presence of mind, the reassuring
words he spoke from the desk, and the self-control
of the singer, who went on singing and did not make
his habitual mistake. At the end Mahler tapped him
on the shoulder, saying with a laugh: 'It seems, my
dear X, that we need a fire to make you sing that
phrase correctly!' The kindness of this reprimand
was in sharp contrast to the uncompromising acerbity
he could and often did show when an artistic question
was involved. During a late, possibly the last, rehearsal of a new production, the cast for which had
already been announced, he was entirely dissatisfied
with the performance of the leading singer, a well-
known and popular figure. From the conductor's
desk he said just what he thought. He replaced the
singer, thus exposing him to the public humiliation

of having someone else sing his role at the opening performance.

At other times he could be all kindness and consideration. A member of the company was mortally ill; he was at endless pains to help him financially and otherwise, even getting him a new contract in order to relieve his mind and deceive him about the hopelessness of his condition. Here, of course, artistic considerations were not involved; where they were, as in the earlier case, he was completely 'amoral' and unable even to see that he should have softened the blow. Once in an endeavour to get him not to be so ruthless, I discussed a case of this kind with him, only to receive the unforgettable, and really naive, reply: 'Look here, once the first unpleasantness is over, I am immediately good again!' He simply could not see that the other fellow was entitled to feel badly about it, or that weaker natures could not accept the strict line he drew between the moral and the artistic.

In his beautiful farewell letter to the members of the Opera, he said that 'under the pressure of the fight, in the heat of the moment, neither I nor you have escaped hurts and mistakes.' Now, when the Mahler period and the contribution of its artists has achieved an almost legendary stature, it can be seen how much was at stake, and what a significant and determinant battle was actually won. And Mahler never treated anyone else as ruthlessly as he treated himself. At every rehearsal he demanded the utmost of himself, and never spared himself, even when he was ill. It is well-nigh inconceivable that he should have written his Fourth, Fifth, Sixth, Seventh, and Eighth symphonies and a series of songs with orchestra during the brief summer vacations of his years as director, and that for ten years he only exchanged the immense burden of directing the Opera for the greater burden of creative work. His life was an artistic cycle: he poured his energy into art and received it back renewed from art. Except in my very last years in Vienna, I never saw him other than vivid, inspired, bursting with vitality.

His working day began early, at home, with a couple of hours at his desk orchestrating his latest work. Then he walked to the Opera and dealt with correspondence and business until rehearsal time. At midday we would often go out together, and I would accompany him, often after a stroll in the Stadtpark, to his home in the Auenbruggerstrasse. Sometimes we would meet in a café in the afternoon; sometimes there were stimulating evenings at his home or with friends. There were unforgettable evenings, too, at restaurants after his glorious first nights; the job done, he would discuss it in detail. I revelled in his talk, it was always suggestive and stimulating, the outcome of a mind forever on the move. Nevertheless, it seems to me that in Vienna, with his intense preoccupations and all the responsibilities a director has to carry, the tone of his talk was in general less aimed at the heights, less transcendental and more worldly. Yet even when speaking of day-to-day matters, he never lost the 'above-the-battle' attitude of the artist whose home is not here, but in the realm of art, and who carries his isolation about with him. Metaphysical questions would suddenly, abruptly arise in his mind and in his talk. An inner *basso ostinato* could be overlaid but never silenced. Every contact with his creative work, whether at his own desk in the morning or in its production in Vienna or elsewhere, would remove his gaze from the day's pressing demands and turn it towards his inner life.

His Fourth Symphony, begun in the summer of 1899, was completed in 1900. In December 1901 it was performed in Munich and fiercely attacked. I was not present, and only learned from a friend how badly things had gone. The first Vienna performance, in 1902, I recall vividly; the explosion of contrary opinions was so violent that fisticuffs ensued between opponents and enthusiasts. In Vienna, Mahler won his place as a creative artist very slowly. While the musical public was almost unanimously devoted to his conducting, it was for a number of years largely opposed to his compositions. The year 1902, however, was to bring the victory of his life with the triumphant reception of his Third Symphony at the Krefeld Music Festival—a victory that had lengthy repercussions. From that day on, other conductors became interested, they performed his works, he was an accepted composer. The *première* of his Fifth Symphony in Cologne stands out in my memory for a special reason; it was the first, and, I believe, the only, occasion when the performance of a work of Mahler's under his own baton left me dissatisfied. The orchestration failed to bring out clearly the complicated contrapuntal tissue of the voices. Mahler himself said plaintively to me afterwards that it seemed to him he never would be able to master the orchestral treatment. Indeed, he later revised the orchestration more drastically than he ever did before or afterwards in any other work. The reception was, I recall, highly enthusiastic, showing how the composer's status was rising in general esteem.

Mahler always presented a stoical front to approval or disapproval; the embattled reception of his Fourth Symphony in Vienna left his withers unwrung, and while the success of the Third Symphony in Krefeld pleased him, he was wholly unaffected by the heady wine of success. This made it really shattering to see him reduced almost to tears by the adverse verdict of a very prominent musician on his Sixth, the so-called 'Tragic' Symphony. No similar experience comes to my mind, and I am sure that the gloomy cast of the work itself had a good deal to do with this most unusual sensitiveness on his part. In general, critical praise or blame left him unaffected. On the morning after the performance of one of his works or of an important production at the Opera, he would say jokingly: 'Well, what have our superiors to say?' and receive the report with unruffled calm. One of my happiest memories is of a concert to which the Verein der schaffenden Tonkünstler, of which I was a member, had invited him;

he responded with warmth to the reverence then shown him by such younger composers as Schönberg and Zemlinsky.

The evening, devoted entirely to songs with orchestra, was really a Mahler Festival; it took place in the Kleiner Musikvereinsaal, and the executants were excellent singers from the Opera and a chamber combination from his Philharmonic. It was a happy evening; the devotion of these young musicians meant more to him than the noisy plaudits of a great audience: their hearts responded to his own in the message that his songs conveyed. The impression he made on such occasions on gifted, eager young artists like these was wholly sympathetic: he was full of interest and outflowing kindness.

In personal intercourse the key to his heart was talent and high endeavour. I do not believe that anyone who was gifted and of a serious turn of mind ever met his harsher side. He was, however, far too much a child of nature ever to feel at home in what is called 'Society'. Its conventions, conversation, and formalities put him off; to what was authentic, genuine, spiritual, he responded instinctively. In company, he was an intimidating element, and he avoided it as far as he could. When he was in good spirits and feeling conversational, he would be the centre of a cheerful group; but if he was upset, such a thundercloud brooded over the gathering that only he could dispel it.

While he could be outgiving, sympathetic, and helpful, he was also capable of a quite staggering

lack of consideration for others. One day as we were
leaving the Opera we were joined by a musician
whom, as a rule, he liked, but whom at that moment
he did not want to see. In the middle of a sentence
from him Mahler, without a word of explanation or
farewell, dashed to catch a tram and was gone. He did
not mean to be rude: he merely escaped, instinctively, from what was for the moment an unwelcome
conversation. Again, one hot day in June, a composer
came to play his opera for him. I came in towards
the end of the last act to find composer and director
in shirt-sleeves; the composer was bathed in sweat;
Mahler was obviously sunk in an abyss of boredom
and distaste. He did not utter a single word; the
composer, incensed by his silence, also said nothing.
I saw no way to save the situation. Finally, the composer put on his coat, picked up his score, and after
a few more moments of painful silence, ended the
uncomfortable scene with an *'Au revoir!'* of chill
politeness. A crowded life of every kind of personal
contact had not endowed Mahler with that minimum
of *savoir faire* needed to wind up this encounter
normally. Yet, when his feelings were touched, he
could be both polite and obliging. His bearing and
manner were those of a well-bred man of the world.
But he was stiff-necked and showed it in his ordinary
contacts, in public, and with officials. Indeed, it says
much for these last that they had enough respect for
a great artist and a self-willed individual to support
him through thick and thin. But it is not surprising
if, at the end of ten years during which his enemies

in the press and the official world had been hard at work, the ground had been dug from under his feet.

I cannot now recall the final reason for his resignation; it was, anyhow, only the final drop that made the bucket overflow. Shortly before it happened, Mahler, jogging his chair back and forwards as he spoke, said in his caustic way: 'This is my present case. If I want to stay put, I have only to lean back firmly to hold my place. But I am making no resistance, so I shall go down in the end.' Soon after this he called me out of rehearsal one day at noon. We left the Opera together and I can see him now as we walked down the Ringstrasse and I heard him say in a calm and gentle tone of voice that he had resigned. I recall his admirable words: 'In these ten years at the Opera, I have fulfilled my cycle.' In the deeper sense, he was right. His artistic task at the Opera was completed; it must now give place to his own last great works and to the settlement of his own problems. We spoke, I remember, of his future plans, of the work in America that would provide a comfortable livelihood and a quieter life, and so on. When I got home I was moved to write him a serious letter about what had happened; he acknowledged it in a few, very beautiful lines.

Far more serious and disturbing was what he told me in the autumn of this same year, again as we walked along the Ringstrasse. His doctor had suddenly discovered that his heart was seriously affected. As he spoke I recalled an incident during a rehearsal of *Lohengrin* which had troubled me at the time. He found a lack of vigour in the delivery and action of the swan chorus; to show what he wanted at the point where '*Ein Wunder* . . .' begins, he seized two members of the chorus by the hands, and with an expression of enthusiastic excitement, dragged them half across the stage towards King Henry. I had often seen him, in this sort of way, stimulating the chorus to incredible feats. This time, however, he suddenly let their hands go and stood, deathly pale and motionless, with his own hand on his heart. I imagine that he then, for the first time, felt his heart deficiency. Now he spoke of the serious consequences of the discovery of his illness and of the revolutionary change in his life and work which would result from the precautions he would have to take from then on. Accustomed to relying on long walks, even on mountain-climbing, for the inspiration of his music, he had now to restrict all bodily movement as much as possible. This discipline entailed not only a heavy sacrifice, but anxiety about his work. Even more important, however, than the serious but inevitable changes in his working habits, seemed to me the marked shift in his whole outlook. The mystery of death had always been in his mind and thoughts; now it was within sight; his world, his life lay under the sombre shadow of its proximity. The tone of our talk was unsentimental and ˈrealistic'; behind it I felt the darkness that had overspread his being. 'I shall,' he said, 'soon get used to it.' *Das Lied von der Erde* and the Ninth Symphony, both composed after his illness, are eloquent witness to the courage with which he strove, and to his success.

In October 1907 he took leave of the Opera with a performance of *Fidelio*; and, in November, of his Vienna friends with one of his Second Symphony. Their tributes of love, devotion, and sorrow at his departure gladdened and moved him.

A great epoch in the history of opera was closed —the achievements of one man and of the fellow workers whom he had inspired. Every one of us had learned from him; from every one of us he had obtained the best. The manifestations of his artistry created the unforgotten glorious period of the Vienna Opera; the integrity of will that raised it to such heights is a lasting example.

V

LAST YEARS

In December 1907 Mahler went to America for the first time. The hour of his departure was early, but hundreds of people were at the station to bid him farewell as he left Vienna. A strenuous time awaited him, but he felt release as he looked back over ten years' responsibility for the Vienna Opera. At the Metropolitan in New York he would not have to take on new tasks, let alone cope with new problems, but would only be employing resources already available there for the production of works that he knew well. While his concert activities in 1909–10, and again in 1910–11, represented a great responsibility and made great demands on his strength, they were limited in either case to half of the year.

In the last years of his life I saw him but rarely. Instead of the almost constant intercourse of the preceding six years, we had but little time together —a few weeks when he was in Vienna, between the winter's conducting in New York and summer work in Toblach; the days of the first performance, in Prague, of his Seventh Symphony, and of the Eighth in Munich; finally, a few hours in Paris—the last we were to have. Vivid in my mind are the sunny autumn days in Prague. The place recalled experiences of his young days as a young conductor at the Landestheater; the rehearsals and performance of the Seventh Symphony of course provided us with many occasions for lively discussion. He was satisfied with its instrumentation; we knew that every measure told. We made an expedition by car into the pleasant countryside; we talked together or in groups of friends and family; perfect harmony prevailed.

Then in the winter of 1909–10 Emil Gutmann, the concert manager, made arrangements for a performance of the Eighth Symphony which Mahler at first awaited with some apprehension. Gutmann, without consulting him, had advertised a performance of 'The Symphony of the Thousand'. Mahler described the affair as a 'Barnum and Bailey Show' and foresaw all sorts of troubles and difficulties in the organization of its massive effects. At his wish I had chosen and rehearsed the soloists. When he got to Vienna, early in 1910, he sat in on a rehearsal that took place at my home. As we began, a fearful thunderstorm broke out and we had to keep interrupting our work. He patiently accepted this sabotage by the heavens. He murmured approval of the soloists, and I could see the effect on all concerned of this gentleness on the part of the man of wrath. Satisfied next with the choral work, he departed for Toblach, coming to Munich at the beginning of September.

Those were great days for us who shared in the

rehearsals of the Eighth. The hand of the master controlled the vast array without apparent effort. All concerned, including the children, who adored him at once, were filled with a solemn elevation of mood. What a moment it was, when at the zenith of his career, and, little as we knew it, soon to be called from us by the hand of fate, he took his place amid the applause of the thousands filling the vast auditorium, in front of the one thousand performers—above all at the point where the *Creator spiritus*, whose fire inspired him, is called on and a thousand voices utter the cry expressing his whole life's longing— *Accende lumen sensibus, infunde amorem cordibus!* As the last note died away and a storm of applause surged towards him, Mahler stepped up to where, at the top of the platform, the chorus of children stood. He went along the line shaking their outstretched hands as they cheered him. This tribute of love from the young filled him with hope for the future of his work and gave him deep joy.

During rehearsals his friends had anxiously noted many signs of physical weakness. But at the performance he seemed at the height of his powers. The lift of his spirit gave his tired heart its old vigour. This was, however, the last time he conducted a composition of his own; he never heard his last two works.

When he first spoke to me of *Das Lied von der Erde*, he called it a 'Symphony in Songs'. It was planned to be his Ninth. Then he changed his mind. He thought of how, for Beethoven and for Bruckner, a ninth symphony had written *finis*; he hesitated to challenge fate. He gave me the manuscript to study; it was the first time that I learned to know a new work of his otherwise than through himself. When I brought it back, well-nigh incapable of uttering a word, he turned to the *Abschied*, saying: 'What do you think? Is it at all bearable? Will it drive people to make an end of themselves?' Then, indicating the rhythmic difficulties, he said jestingly: 'Have you any notion how this should be conducted? I haven't!'

If my memory serves me, he never himself gave me the score of the Ninth, for which, being a symphony, the ominous number was unavoidable. I see from one of his letters that in the autumn of 1909 he took it with him to New York 'in almost illegible form', in the hope of producing a fair copy there. He must have taken it back to Vienna early in 1910, but I do not recall ever seeing it there; it was only after his death that it came into my hands. It may be that a superstitious shrinking from a Ninth prevented his talking to me about it. Yet in that clear and powerful mind I had never detected any trace of superstition. Nor can there have been anything of the sort here; he knew only too well what the Fates had in store.

Although I actually saw little of him in the last years of his life, I was compensated for this loss by the intensity of his communication by letter and the profundity of our conversations. As in nature, twilight dissolves in the glow of sunset, the gloom thrown on his spirit at the onset of his illness passed into the mild radiance of approaching departure, lending a new loveliness to the 'dear Earth' whose chant he had composed, and seeming to cast a secret shimmer over his speech and writing. I shall never forget his expression as he told me that he had never found the world so beautiful as on a recent visit to the Bohemian countryside and as he spoke of the delicious fragrance rising from the soil. Deep emotional turmoil lay behind his talk. Touching on a wide range of intellectual topics, as in the Hamburg days, it reached out constantly to metaphysical issues, and with a higher and more ardent pressure than of old. His mood might have been likened to a sort of travel fever of the soul, interrupted now and then by passages of serene calm: we even talked of plans for the future. We spoke of a house and garden on the Hohe Warte or in Grinzing, and of a *Kaffeehaus* where we might meet of an afternoon. But such idyllic flights of fancy were likely to end in a gesture or glance of disbelief.

A singular grim incident, which happened, I believe, during his last summer, depressed him deeply. He told me that while working in his composition cottage at Toblach he was suddenly startled by an incomprehensible noise. Something 'frightfully dark' burst through the window, and proved, when he rose in horror, to be an eagle that filled the small space with its hurtlings to and fro. The dread apparition was brief; the eagle stormed away as swiftly as it had come. Then when Mahler dropped, exhausted, on the sofa, a crow flew out from under it. His

musical heaven had become a battlefield for one of
the endless fights of 'all against all'. His story reflected the horror of this immediate demonstration
of nature's awful cruelty, which had always lain at
the root of the deep sorrow in his soul; the incident
had brought it all to the surface again.

In the autumn of 1910 he returned to New York;
in February 1911 came the news that he was gravely
ill. When he went to Paris in April for a serum treatment I determined to go and see him there. There
he lay, the tormented victim of an unpredictable
disease that now affected his spirit as well as his
body. His mood was bleak and aloof. When, in an
effort to turn his mind to more cheerful subjects,
I spoke of his work, his response was wholly pessimistic for the first time. I therefore avoided serious
topics and simply tried to distract his mind by talk
on other, unrelated subjects. I was not wholly un-
successful; indeed, I recall that my report of some
remarks on the subject of art, made by a well-known
Philistine, produced a faint smile in which there was
a tinge of the old sense of humour. Another incident
gave a gleam of the same kind; he wanted to be
shaved—a youthful French barber appeared who
seemed to combine the whole elegance of his nation
with that of his profession. While he plied his craft
with exaggerated delicacy I caught something like a
flicker of amusement in the sick man's eye. He may
have recalled the fantastic barber of some fairy tale.
When the young man had bowed himself out,
Mahler looked after him, murmuring softly, but in

a lively tone: 'Farewell, beard-scraper!' In my efforts to distract him I often failed; his immobile face showed how far away he was. When I tried to describe the future house and garden about which we had often spoken in Vienna, he did not answer immediately and then gave me a sad reply: 'That would be nice, but my only desire now is to be allowed enough digitalis to keep my heart going.' Then, his mood would change; he listened with interest to everything I could tell him about Vienna and what was going on in the musical world there. While he often showed resentment, the old attachment broke through frequently; at bottom he enjoyed nothing so much as stories of that world he knew so well. I had to leave after a few days. We had no more talk. When I next saw him he was dying.

In May he was carried to Vienna. No bitterness born of the manifold disappointments of his time there could prevail against his desire to 'come home' at the last. He found joy in the friendly greetings and signs of devotion that greeted him on all sides. On May 18, 1911, he died. Next evening as we laid the coffin in the cemetery at Grinzing, a storm broke and such torrents of rain fell that it was almost impossible to proceed. An immense crowd, dead silent, followed the hearse. At the moment when the coffin was lowered, the sun broke through the clouds.

REFLECTION

I

THE OPERA DIRECTOR

MAHLER'S dramatic talent equalled his musical gifts; this was the reason for his greatness as an opera director. He was as much at home on the stage as with the score. He could breathe his own fiery glow into the dramatic action as into the musical performance and get his artists to meet the demands, representational or musical, of any given work.

His personality was dramatic; he was a man of intense feeling and imagination. He could enter into Alberich's despair when the Ring is snatched from him, and share the frenzy of the curse he hurls at those who rob him of it; he breathed with Pizarro's prisoners in their brief spell of release; he knew the jealous rage that fills Mr. Ford when he believes that his wife's lover is hidden in the laundry-basket; he was Wotan as he curbs Brünnhilde's disobedience, and Brünnhilde as she seeks to soften her father's wrath. Nothing human, nothing divine, was alien to him: Beckmesser's petty spite was not too low, nor the St. John's Day mood of Hans Sachs too lofty for him. He lived in everything, and everything lived in him. However remote an action or sentiment, however foreign to his own character, he could enter into it imaginatively as into the mind of any man, in any situation. As he sat in the orchestra pit his heart was on the stage; his conducting, or rather, his music-making, was governed by the drama.

When, as a young assistant conductor, I went from Pressburg to Vienna I heard him conduct a performance of *Lohengrin* which set me a permanent standard. In the scene outside the cathedral, where Elsa and Ortrud are quarrelling, I suddenly realized the essential nature of opera. Mahler was not just conducting the orchestral accompaniment to a contralto song: he was with Ortrud in spirit: he *was* Ortrud; he was transporting both orchestra and singer into the heart of a deeply humiliated woman—at the same time his music took in Elsa's terror and her profound belief in Lohengrin. His conducting penetrated to the soul of the music, and directly to its dramatic essence. This scene from *Lohengrin* was a simple case; here music as such has no independent life of its own because Wagner assigns it an almost exclusively dramatic function. The so-called 'Mystery Ensemble' is another matter. Even here, however, while the music has more independent significance, the essence is still dramatic, centring as it does on Lohengrin's bewilderment, Elsa's doubts, the varying attitudes taken by others, all overarched by a sense of approaching catastrophe which must find expression in the music. More exacting demands have here to be met: the spirit of the music and of the drama must be expressed simultaneously.

Another profoundly moving experience rounded

off the lesson of *Lohengrin*. At the opening of the second act of *Figaro* the first bars of the Countess's aria transported one into the realm of absolute music; the song of the strings and the voice of the singer alike dwelt there; the theatre vanished, overwhelmed; the Countess's pain and longing were resolved in the higher sphere of music. One did not feel in any sense removed into the concert hall, but 'lost to this world' and to that of the theatre. Mahler had conjured the very spirit of music until it held unchallenged sway; and how this spirit overflowed both audience and performers as he evoked it in the shimmering reconciliation passages that precede the presto at the close of the fourth act!

Opera as an art form lives between the two poles I have here tried to indicate. Mahler was its master from pole to pole. He knew when music should unfold its full power and submerge drama; he knew, too, when and in what degree it had to subserve it —when the dramatic aspect should be uppermost.

Understanding as he did how to dramatize music, he also strove to infuse drama with the spirit of music—the most taxing problem in opera. His musical interpretation communicated to his singers the power of dramatic expression. This was not all. Gesture and movement are part of dramatic representation; he used music to infuse and guide that representation. I am not here thinking of mere pantomimic response, as in the string passages accompanying Beckmesser's scrawlings or lending expressive force to the silent play of feeling between Siegmund

and Sieglinde. What I have in mind is an interpenetration by music of the mood of any significant
scene; an interpenetration providing for the finer
shades of expression—a glance, a smile—and allow-
ing no gesture to break the musical texture. He was
able to penetrate the heart of the music and realize,
within himself, the composer's dramatic vision.
Here his own notable histrionic gifts came to his aid;
he could show, not merely say, how a given scene
should be played in consonance with the music.
His will was evoked to a full realization of the
author's intentions. But it is only Wagner and works
of the post-Wagnerian period that show any 'pre-
established harmony' between what is in the score
and what is taking place on the stage. Mozart also
wrote dramatic music, but no scenic directions in
his scores, consequently there were no indications
for Mahler to go by. Anyone, however, who saw
Mahler's *Figaro* will recall how subtly and vividly
the comedy of the stage was made to correspond
with the spirit of the music. One example may
serve—the exquisite way in which the music led the
action of the page in Susanna's aria '*Venite inginoc-
chiatevi.*'

In rehearsal Mahler was guided by intuition and
impulse, not by any fixed method or principle. He
knew the work by heart. He had a picture of it.
Here was the stage, here were gifted artists. His
imagination in a happy glow, he drew inspiration
from the dramatic situation, illumination from the
score. When he had to deal with artists of talent,

his demands rose; when they were inadequate, he would use gentler methods of getting the best out of them. Always he was the imaginative servant of the work of art itself. Never was he tempted by the abundance of his powers to 'play his own hand'.

Complete unity was the goal he set himself: a mutual interaction of score and stage. He grew to see that such unity was not achieved merely by the fusion of action and music; staging, costume, and lighting had to be brought up to an equal pitch of perfection. At a significant juncture he met Alfred Roller, who had reached the same conclusion from the point of view of the painter. Roller's sets for *Tristan* showed deep visual understanding; thenceforth Mahler and Roller worked together for the realization of his ideal of unity in operatic performance. Up to then it had been assumed that it was enough to have stage décor, costumes, and lighting that satisfied broadly cultivated tastes and were an interesting contribution towards the production; the idea of integrating music and drama and infusing them both with a dominating idiom and mood was in its infancy, in so far as it existed at all. Roller, a painter of imagination steeped in the theatre and its possibilities, was, like Mahler, filled with the desire for animation of the opera stage. His decorative use of three-dimensional settings greatly increased the effectiveness of his lighting, which in turn became an element in the suggestive power both of the drama and of the music. The colours and forms he employed were organically related to the mood of the work; even his costumes played their part. An indescribably moving performance of *Tristan* ushered in the great period in Mahler's search for perfection.

His aims were complex and novel. His approach suggested that he was experimenting and gave rise to much public discussion and excitement, more especially because breaking new ground inevitably involved mistakes and imperfections. The most constructive re-creation of this period, his *Don Giovanni*, was obviously experimental, and became the target of lively critical comment. He had the admirable idea of creating a fixed stage frame to facilitate rapid changes of scene; its drawback was that its turrets did not automatically, or even naturally, fit any particular scene. The colours, again, were too strong for the mild glow of Mozart's orchestration; the choice of singer for the leading role proved unfortunate. Nevertheless, the performance as a whole demonstrated clearly the problem Mahler and Roller tried to solve; with all its failings, it can now be seen as showing the way to the most interesting and promising productions of its time. Each subsequent production profited by the ones that had gone before, until that of Gluck's *Iphigenia in Aulis* scaled heights unique in my experience.

Mahler never relaxed his pioneer effort to secure unified performances of opera in which all the elements would be spiritually fused. He knew how to lift his artists to heights of achievement, where personal impact and obedience to the demands of the work, adaptation to the whole, and unfolding of individuality were all linked together. In his own contribution, absolute loyalty to the work—which alone concerned him—was married to the freedom proper to genius. Dramatic interpretation demands a wider imaginative scope than pure music, for the theatre has developed no technique of written instructions which could be compared with the accuracy of a musical score. Even Wagner's plastic vision of the dramatic action, expressed as it is in full stage directions, leaves much open to interpretation. This very fact imposes on a stage director's conscience an obligation to select among the possibilities open to his imagination those essential to the work as a whole, underlining them at the expense of what is inessential so as to preserve continuity of style. Mahler's interpretations were a model of this wider view of loyalty to the work.

In his view, changes were permissible only when lack of clarity in the original makes business on the stage hard to interpret, or when the author's intentions might be compromised by an easily remediable imperfection in direction. Mozart and Wagner were, in general, sacrosanct. In *Figaro*, however, he enlarged the court scene in order to clarify the significance of Marcellina's suit against Figaro. Of course he did not alter a note; he merely expanded the *secco* recitative. In the same way, there was an interesting, if belated, justification for his small infringement on Goetz's *Taming of the Shrew*. He struck out the closing scenes, and made the opera end with the beautiful duet between Petruchio and Katharina.

Although this proved highly successful with audiences, he was troubled, feeling that a conductor had no right to deal thus with another man's work. It was an immense relief to his sensitive conscience to discover that Goetz, arranging a piano score for a performance in Mannheim, had made precisely the same change.

It goes without saying that outside the works of the great masters—Mozart, Beethoven, Weber, Gluck, Wagner—he felt a freedom, and indeed an obligation, to put his rich experience at the service of the composer. Operas such as *The Tales of Hoffmann*, *La Dame Blanche*, *The Merry Wives of Windsor*, *La Juive*, and *The Taming of the Shrew* profited by this; the more so as he used such freedom solely in the interest of securing performances that fully realized their creators' dreams. About these he knew no doubt once his intuition had penetrated into the artist's workshop. It was indeed this intimate knowledge of the author's intentions which gave to his interpretations, for all their daring, the impression of assurance and authenticity. He had no trace of vanity, no desire for merely theatrical effect. The work itself was, for him, the law. His performances, and the Opera under him, were governed by this sense of dedication.

II

THE CONDUCTOR

'THE works, beyond description glorious, are bright, as on the earliest day'. So, in *Faust*, the Archangel sings of God's creations. Mahler's reverence for the great works of music was of this exalted order. 'Bright as on the earliest day' he felt them. Thus they sounded under his baton. Thus he made audiences hear them. A sense of something done for the first time, with first intention, spontaneous, was the chief characteristic in his interpretations.

Only penetration into the depth of the great creations of art, as well as those of nature, reveals that element of ultimate immeasurability which is the hallmark of greatness. Only he who enters deeply enough into the work to feel this can always arouse fresh interest and enthusiasm, while the superficial mind, which assumes that it understands all about a given work, knows it through and through, is likely to lose freshness and relapse into routine performance. Intimate knowledge strengthened Mahler's wonder and admiration for works 'beyond description glorious', fed and renewed his first intention. He approached them like a lover, constantly wooing;

he was always ready to reconsider, improve, plumb new depths. Nothing was routine in his performances; even if he was giving a work for the thirtieth time, he gave it as though for the first. Though his approach seemed free and impetuous, it was invariably governed by the most rigorous exactitude. He observed and demanded from all who worked with him, complete faithfulness to the score, its notation, tempos, agogic marks, and dynamics. Even the singers had to sing by the books; he was never content until absolute precision had been achieved 'above and below'—on the stage and in the orchestra. The transparency of his conducting responded to his demand for absolute musical clarity. The precision of his exemplary beat was never impaired by emotion, however strong. At the innumerable performances I attended, I heard mistakes by singers and instrumentalists, but never any failure in precision or ensemble: the unfailing certainty of his beat always kept singers and orchestra together. But one never had the impression of mechanical precision, nor can I recall an occasion when audience or critics even mentioned his accuracy. With him, precision was a means to an end, the end being to bring the work to life. Talents, however high, were, if not controlled by a well-nigh pedantic sense of form, dismissed as mere sound and fury; only when his fiery hold over singers and orchestra had established an absolute clarity of interpretation did he permit himself the free flight of spirit which gave his performances the effect of improvisation.

His interpretation was never arbitrary. That he was accused of this was owing to the wide difference between his inspired renderings and what audiences were used to. When he made changes in the classics, they were designed to make the spirit live rather than reproduce the dead letter. Hence his much criticized retouching of the instrumentation of Beethoven's Ninth and other works in which, knowing as he did the resources of the modern orchestra, he used them to clarify and realize Beethoven's intentions. When attacked on this ground in Vienna he defended his action in a public statement in which he drew attention to the contrast between the power of Beethoven's conception and the limited instrumental capacities in Beethoven's day. He cited the example of Wagner and stressed the obligation on the conductor to let the voices soar out clearly.

I have noted his fanatical devotion to the score; it never blinded him to the paramount duty of realizing the composer's intentions. Now most people accept modifications of this kind, though there are still differences as to how they should be effected. In Mahler's case, they derived from his amazing ear for the inner meaning, even when contemporary instrumentation left it obscure. 'Your Beethoven is not my Beethoven,' he grunted to a well-meaning friend who took him to task for unfamiliar renderings. So in truth it was; he knew Beethoven by direct experience, and his performance of him was an experience. His Beethoven had nothing in common with the smooth classic presented in so many routine

performances. His *Fidelio*, his Third 'Leonora' Overture, and his indescribable *Coriolanus* Overture are
vivid enough in my memory for me to testify to his
spiritual kinship with the real Beethoven. He had
within him his thunderstorms, his power, his love.
Scrupulous as he was for detail, he had also the simplicity, the truthfulness, and the symphonic understanding that respect the primary claim of organic
form.

Arbitrary or subjective renderings were incompatible with his penetrating divination of the depths
of a work. The picture in his mind's eye was complete; there were no gaps to fill. The real explanation of arbitrary alteration and subjective transformation is sometimes mere pretentiousness and a craving
for originality, more often the imperfection of the
interpreter's vision, his lack of the seeing eye, of
the penetrating divination which can reach the heart
of a work. The poor man, eager not to appear shal-
low, has to compensate for his defects with his own
meagre resources.

Clarity ruled Mahler's interpretation of masterpieces. But it was not daylight clarity. Music is no
daytime art; it does not yield its secret roots or its
ultimate depths to the unshadowed soul. It comes
out of the dark, and must be understood and felt in
the dark; it is akin to the sombre heave of the
ocean, not to the clear blue of the Mediterranean.
Darkness surged in Mahler's soul; his eye, native to
the night, was born to realize the depths of music.

'The best in music,' he used to say, 'is not set

down in the notes.' This best, this essential soul leaped forth with such passion from his conducting, with such an effect of personal confession, such elemental force, as to cause occasional doubt as to whether the composer was speaking or Mahler, whose stormy spirit compelled the voice of another to utter his own feeling.

Mahler's sole desire was indubitably to reveal the ultimate depths probed by another—in fact, the work itself. To ask whether interpretation such as his reveals the soul of the interpreter, or of the composer, or a mingling of the two, is to confront the very mystery of musical re-creation. In art, as in life, the fully personal voice, the complete 'I', alone carries conviction and moves us to the depths. The well-meant but mediocre interpretation fails by never establishing identity between interpreter and composer. Not so with the genuine interpreter, whose enthusiastic abandon carries him over into a state where he is 'beside himself'. Then, ecstasy transcends individualism, and the re-creation of another becomes almost creation in its own right. Then, his talent becomes like that of Proteus; heart and imagination, flooded by 'the other', generate a kind of fusion; the barriers between creator and re-creator seem to disappear, and the conductor might be conducting a work of his own. Then, he can speak as 'I', feel as 'I', and this 'I-feeling' gives his interpretation immediacy, complete compulsion. So, in perfect re-creation, loyalty and freedom coincide. To understand that Beethoven's Ninth when

conducted by Richard Wagner was filled with the
spirit of Beethoven, but also alive with Wagner's
personality—moreover, that the full expression of
Wagner's individuality was necessary to set Beethoven's spirit free—is to know the meaning of
musical interpretation.

Mahler's conducting was of this order. His powerful personality was wholly dedicated to revealing the
work of another in all its clarity and strength; it was
his joy to unite two spirits in such performances.

There are cases where difficulty of understanding
and an alien approach impair entry into the mind of
another. Even then, however, neither personal feeling nor a dominating 'I' justifies distortion. Even of
unsympathetic works, Mahler, often to the amaze-
ment of their composers, who knew the gulf between
them and him, gave performances that were at once
faithful to the composer and true to himself. What
matters in such case is a direction of will towards the
'other'; this, as interpreter, he never lacked. Where
there is such a sense of service, the scholastic dictum
quoted by Jean-Paul—'Forty thousand angels can sit
upon the point of a needle'—applies. The structure
of a genuine work of art permits without contraction
of its scope, any and every expression of the interpreter's imagination. There can, indeed, be no convincing performance unless this kind of spiritual
collaboration exists.

As years went on, the picture Mahler presented
on the podium was simplified. Böhler's excellent
silhouettes, drawn in his first period in Vienna,

show him in fierce, violent movement at the desk. He always sat to conduct, but in his first Vienna years, as in Hamburg, his mobility was astounding. But his movements were not excessive or superfluous —they seemed rather like some kind of fanatical conjuration. Gradually posture and gestures became quieter. The spirit behind his technique developed to a point at which he had no difficulty in securing a combination of force and precision by an apparently simple beat, almost without moving his body. A glance, a rare gesture would keep singers and players under his spell without any of the agitation in which he formerly indulged. In his last period in Vienna, the picture was one of almost uncanny calm, with no loss in intensity of effect. I remember a performance of Strauss's *Symphonia Domestica* in which the contrast between the wild storms in the orchestra and the immobility of the conductor who unleashed them made an almost ghostly impression.

At stage rehearsal with orchestra, despite intense preoccupation with purely musical matters, the dramatist in him was Argus-eyed; nothing that happened on the stage escaped his vigilance—action, lighting, and costumes were under perpetual observation. Through example and precept, sometimes tranquil, sometimes vehement, he got the result he wanted. Not because he wanted it, but because he had to get it. His own tremendous 'must' exacted obedience from all who worked with him.

I want, however, to stress once more the fact that the decisive quality of his conducting and the source of its power was the warmth of his heart. That gave his interpretation the impressiveness of a personal message. That rendered unnoticeable the meticulous study lying behind the result he achieved: its virtuosity and accomplishment; that made his music-making what it was—a spontaneous greeting from soul to soul. Here, in the borderland between art and humanity, the nobility and potency of his mind were revealed. The secret of his lasting fame as conductor and director is his ideal combination of high artistic gifts with the ardent sensibility of a great heart.

III

THE COMPOSER

THE fundamental element in Mahler's work is the simple fact that he was a genuine musician. At first he was a romantic at heart—witness *Das klagende Lied* and the *Lieder eines fahrenden Gesellen*—but his later development shows conflict between, and blending of romantic and classical elements. Classical is the determination to give form to the music that gushed from him, to control and master his virile power, imagination, and sensibility. Romantic, in the wider sense, is the bold and unbounded range of his fantasy: his 'nocturnal' quality; a tendency to excess in expression, at times reaching the grotesque; above all, the mixture of poetic and other ideas in his musical imagination. His was a turbulent inner world of music, impassioned humanism, poetic imagination, philosophic thought, and religious feeling. As he had both a feeling heart and the urge and power of ardent expression, he was able to subject his individual musical language to the tyranny of symphonic form. This form came to dominate his creative activity; he was to expand a content, at first rich, various, and dispersed, to the point of chaos, to the creation of works ever richer and more novel.

His First Symphony, although conceived as a personal credo, already showed how completely he was dedicated to the symphonic idea. From the Second Symphony on, his advance along the symphonic path was more and more conscious and determined, and was characterized by the steady development of movements from a thematic core whose musical completeness is deflected by no poetic idea or musical interjection sacrificing the principle of organic coherence. He was to develop symphonic form and expand its scale immensely, above all in his development sections, where he heightened the use of the motif as created and employed by Beethoven—always keeping the idea of the whole structure in mind when forming the single parts. Here he simply follows in Beethoven's tracks. The glorious, singing quality of many of his themes, like the happy-go-lucky Austrian coloration of his melodies, shows traces of the influence of Schubert and of Bruckner. The choral theme in the Second Symphony, the breadth of its layout, and the traces in it of solemnity, also recall Bruckner. There are echoes of Berlioz, too, in the daring use of bizarre and grotesque means for the purpose of reaching the utmost keenness of expression; he perhaps learned more from the great French genius than from anyone else.

However, there was another ancestor in his family tree: the 'unknown musician', the master of folk song. Many important themes, not only in his songs but also in his symphonies, derive from folk song—

nay, are folk song. The feeling, the idea of the poetry
of the people gave the original impetus that set his
musical imagination going. The folklore of the mercenaries tugged at his heartstrings, and gave birth to
many of his songs. As he had destroyed his earlier
work before I knew him, I do not know either his
'Nordic' Symphony nor the operas and chamber
music of that period. I do not even know whether
they derived from 'folksy' feeling or, as I guess, from
Schumann. The youthful works in the first volume
of his songs for piano certainly show traces of
Schumann's influence, with the single exception of
Hans und Grethe', a song charmingly reminiscent of
the dance music of his German-Bohemian home.
The first major work to reveal Mahler's original
genius derives from folk poetry though it has
nothing to do with the mercenaries; he put
Grimm's tale '*Der singende Knochen*' (The Singing
Bone) into verse to form the basis for *Das klagende
Lied*, a composition for chorus, soloists, and orchestra. The music is inspired and thoroughly original,
full of dramatic and human feeling. There followed
the more subjective *Lieder eines fahrenden Gesellen*, in
which a passionate experience finds aesthetic expression. In either case, his imagination seems to be in
full sympathy with the poetic atmosphere of *Des
Knaben Wunderhorn*, though he did not, in fact, read
the work of Arnim and Brentano till some four years
later. A deep insight into a mind plainly akin to those
of the creators of this masterpiece comes if we realize
the close correspondence between his verses and those

written or collected by Arnim and Brentano; in any collection his and theirs would be indistinguishable. The music to which they are set, like the verses themselves, is tender and simple, folk-song-like in feeling. Here are the roots from which his art grew.

When he finally read the *Wunderhorn*, he must have felt as though he was finding his home. Everything that moved him is there—nature, piety, longing, love, parting, night, death, the world of spirits, the tale of the mercenaries, the joy of youth, childhood jokes, quirks of humour, all pour out, as in his songs. Out of the happy marriage of native poetry and a music intimately related to it was born a series of enchanting works. They reveal a personality of virile cast and strong originality.

Mahler's songs—the earlier with piano, the later with orchestral accompaniments—constitute a refreshingly varied, characteristic, and significant part of his work. Each has the mark of creativity, musical invention; none is a mere piece of emotional declamation. I cannot mention them all, but I do want to glance at the various fields to which they belong, for they illustrate the nature of the man. There are soldiers' songs: some spirited: '*Aus, Aus!*' and '*Trost im Unglück*', some sad: '*Zu Strassburg auf der Schanz*' and '*Der Tambourgesell*'; next, three highly expressive of the nocturnal side of his nature, in which there was a region on which the sun never rose. '*Der Schildwache Nachtlied*' is one of the most impressive vocal compositions of this comparatively early stage. Night itself pervades the talk of boy and girl, the tramp of the evening round, and the foreboding of the ending. '*Wo die schönen Trompeten blasen*' is the most touching of the three—nocturnal, again, in its mood and with a gripping ghostly conclusion. The most impressive of them all is '*Revelge*', unique in its reflection of Mahler's own consanguinity with night and death, as in its inexorable marching rhythms, its ghostly colouring, and the emotional tension that brings us into terrifying contact with his demoniac being. Next, a group of pious songs; '*Urlicht*', an expression of simple faith, quite unlike '*Himmlisches Leben*', in which it is presented as a childhood dream —a mood paralleled in '*Es sangen drei Engel*'. The humorous songs are highly characteristic; '*Selbstgefuhl*', '*Ablösung im Sommer*', and '*Des Antonius von Padua Fischpredigt*'. This last, from which Mahler took the thematic material for the inspired scherzo of his Second Symphony, is a masterpiece of originality and humorous expression, as of formal unity. The droll '*Ablösung im Sommer*' produced the central theme of the scherzo of the Third Symphony. Then, there are lovely folk songs like '*Scheiden und Meiden*', '*Nicht wiedersehen*', and, in pride of place, the fourth song in the *Lieder eines fahrenden Gesellen*, '*Die zwei blauen Augen von meinem Schatz*', which reappears as the moving central section of the Funeral March in the First Symphony. Another significant early vocal work of the folk period is '*Das irdische Leben*'. This belongs to no group. It exists in itself, and he rated it high, as was natural, for the story expresses in its simple yet powerful way the woe of the world which haunted him all his life, and which he grew to express with the mature force of his expanding personality. Moreover, this song is one of the first in which his own musical idiom is fully evident.

The smile of a man with a tendency towards deep gloom has a peculiarly refreshing and infectious quality. There is a special charm in the little group of songs in a cheerful vein, e.g., '*Verlorene Müh*', '*Rheinlegendchen*', and '*Wer hat dies Liedlein erdacht?*'

After his Fourth Symphony, Mahler moved from folklore to classic poetry. He felt, in a sense, akin to Rückert, whose exquisite mastery of language, combined with the truthfulness and simplicity of his feeling, attracted Mahler strongly. His choice of the five most beautiful of Rückert's more than one hundred poems for the cycle *Kindertotenlieder* showed his rare understanding of poetry; the work as a whole is a stirring piece of lyric art. The poems themselves are in no sense folk songs; the music too is far removed from the folk-song style of many of his earlier songs. It has a noble melodic substance, as have the five songs, likewise based on Rückert's poems, which followed. There is in '*Ich atmet' einen linden Duft*' a melodic and poetic jewel; a firm belief in God speaks from '*Um Mitternacht*'; while '*Ich bin der Welt abhanden gekommen*' is deeply moving both as song and as personal confession. A characteristic idiom marks all these songs, and however strong their dramatic expression, Mahler never oversteps the limits of the medium.

His songs with orchestra contain perhaps the most sublime examples of the lofty height he had reached in his orchestration. They are perfect illustrations of an exquisite dynamic relation between voice and orchestra. The symphonist in him found particular pleasure in exercising his craft within the limits of the small apparatus of the lied. Master of interpretation, he would expend loving care on getting exquisite sounds out of a reduced orchestra. The variety and even the contrariety of his compositions in the vocal field impressively foreshadow what he was to achieve in the wider field of the symphony.

Has this rich personality given us music of equal stature? I put the question fairly and squarely: did Mahler possess a 'genuine faculty of musical invention'?

When speaking of his songs I suggested that none of them lacks a musical idea. In a song everything depends on the musical core; in a symphony it is ultimately a question of how the idea is worked out. To put it in a somewhat exaggerated form—in a song the idea is what matters: in a symphony idea is a means to an end. In Mahler's symphonies the thematic material reveals the inspiration of an authentic musician, genuine and sound: one who could not work out a major thematic construction from motifs in themselves paltry or artificial. For the sustained development of his symphonic works he required the continuous stimulus of the inspired idea, of the theme given in blessed moments of insight. In music, in the broad sense of the word, everything depends on invention: both the 'material' and its symphonic development. Mahler's inventive faculty carries, in the first place, the stamp of a personality whose originality no one can deny.

I attach importance to recognition of the mingling of classical and romantic in his thematic material, as in his nature. But where he draws on themes from the sphere of folklore, he never merely imitates, let alone adapts; it is the genuine voice of the people with which he speaks, and which comes from deep within his own being.

The counterpart here is the 'symphonic' theme, in Beethoven's sense: broad in construction, meaningful in substance, which forms the core of symphonic work. The last movement of Mahler's First shows a dominant symphonic theme of this kind, although the movement as a whole is governed by emotion rather than by symphonic design. With the powerful opening measures of the Second, a great symphonic composer begins his work and at the same time continues the great tradition of the classical symphony. The broad layout of the major theme remains characteristic; it was to be further developed and enlarged in the Sixth and Seventh, and, above all, in the Ninth. Like the old masters, he generally sets opposite his main, masculine theme a singing, feminine one. With it folk music is left behind; here is lyricism on the model of the classical second theme. The thematic substance of the slow movements is song—a long-drawn-out, funeral song—as is the case with Bruckner. The same broad thematic layout appears also in the last movements.

The inventiveness shown in his scherzos deserves a word. A musician with his strange sense of humour was bound to produce scherzos of notable, even singular, distinction of invention. A quite special place must be given to the scherzo of the Second, both as a piece of composition and as a specimen of musical inventiveness; it certainly is a high point in symphonic scherzo literature. That of the Third is both droll and charming; that of the Fourth mysterious and exciting. The scherzo of the Fifth is not humorous, but has immense vitality. In the Sixth the trio of the scherzo has a singular and wholly Mahlerish charm. In the Seventh the scherzo is a spooky night-piece; in the Ninth the Austrian country dance is employed with consummate mastery and delicious grace.

In general, Mahler made happy use of the Austrian musical dialect. It sounds in the trio of the second movement of the First, with echoes of Schubert, and with some of Haydn in the main theme of the first movement of the Fourth; there are Styrian touches in the country dance in the Ninth, to which I have already referred. The traditional opening bar of the Austrian military band, played by drums and cymbals, is wittily reproduced in the March of the Third, and its scherzo 'sounds off' in true military fashion. There are echoes of Vienna's folk songs in the secondary theme of the Fourth and even a Viennese waltz in the scherzo of the Fifth; one of

the variations in the andante of the Fourth behaves in a
very Austrian fashion indeed. Austrian military music,
of which he was very fond, permeates his marches.
When he was a two-year-old, his nurse used to leave
him in a barracks yard while she enjoyed the company of a soldier friend: he listened to drums and
trumpets, and watched soldiers marching; the romantic aspect of the military, often present in his
work, may perhaps derive from these infantile barracks impressions. The reveille sounds twice; the
Grosser Appell in the last movement of the Second
symbolizes the call to the dead to rise for the Last
Judgment; the first movement of the Fourth completes the picture, with the finely modulated *Kleiner
Appell*, as he called it. Military, again, are the repeated
trumpets in the introduction to the first movement
of the Third, the wild music of the 'charge', and the
closing march-rhythms on the drums. Military rom-
ance also colours songs like '*Der Schildwache Nachtlied*',
'*Der Tambourgesell*' and '*Revelge*'.

Marches recur in Mahler's work. In his First and
Fifth symphonies, the funeral march carries a singu-
lar, tragic-ironic meaning; in the finale of his
Second, a vigorous quick march plays an important
part. A fiery march—'*Der Sommer marschiert ein*'—
occupies a large portion of the first movement of his
Third. There are march rhythms in the first move-
ment of the Sixth, the second movement of the
Seventh, and the last movements of the Fifth and
Seventh.

With his Second Symphony, Mahler begins to

think in contrapuntal terms. Its polyphonic structure and artful formation and transformation of
motifs show the work's classical affiliation. Mahler's
absorption in problems of technique grew steadily
right up to his Ninth; by the time of the Fifth they
had produced a radical change in his style. Far from
being a poet setting poetic visions to music, he was,
as I said at the opening of this chapter, a musician
pur sang. As such, he was primarily concerned to
achieve his aim by the plastic use of thematic
material. This aim governs the shape of every movement, the development of every theme: the use of
counterpoint, the moulding of rondo, fugue, etc.,
in the sonata form. His first four symphonies are
infiltrated with ideas, images, and emotions. From
the Fifth to the Seventh inclusive, purely musical
forms dominate. Between these two periods, he was
absorbed in Bach; *The Art of the Fugue* had a profound
influence on his counterpoint. This is plain in the
rondo-fugue of the Fifth, in which a tendency to
imaginative deepening of the rondo itself is also
evident. The exalted *Veni, Creator Spiritus* of the
Eighth, like the contrapuntal mastery of the third
movement of the Ninth, dedicated to the 'Brothers
in Apollo', shows immense advance in his polyphony. He was also particularly interested in the art
of variations. He was a passionate admirer of
Brahms's *Variations on a Theme of Haydn* and loved to
explain how high a standard Brahms in this composition had given the whole concept of variations.
Mahler's use of variations is confined to the andante

of his Fifth, but the 'variant'—the transformation and elaboration of a given theme, lying, as it does, at the basis of variation—is a significant element in development, and one by which he was constantly preoccupied. In each of his later symphonies the art of variation is progressively used, and enriches both recapitulation and coda.

There was, also, a notable advance in instrumentation, based in his case on an unrivalled capacity for vivid sound-imagination and on an intimate knowledge of the orchestra. Yet his imaginative mastery of sound never seduced him into attaching too great importance to coloration. He used his rare aural gifts to achieve the utmost orchestral lucidity. Where special colour was needed to fulfil his intentions, he mixed it on his own palette, as only one of his amazing sensibility could do. The heightening of his polyphony, with its complex interweaving of vocal effects, taxed even his instrumental mastery: in his Fifth he himself had difficulty keeping pace with the growing complications of the structure.

Mahler's instrumentation deserves study. A theoretical analysis of his progress in expanding the idea of the symphony, and of the development of his polyphony, his harmony, his thematic style, his technique of variation, could be rewarding. This, however, is no place for such a professional study. It is a task a young composer would find well worth his while.

His work forms a musical whole, with no gaps in musically logical continuity or structure. And yet no evaluation in strictly musical terms can be just, for his work was the outcome of his entire inner life. It has to be viewed as the expression in music of a great spirit. Human as well as aesthetic values must enter in, if his creative significance is to be realized. I propose to look at the part played by his experience, his cast of thought, his poetic vision, and his religious feeling in each of his symphonies, for in each it is unique. One word in advance: if 'programme music' is the musical description of extra-musical processes, he never wrote it.

His First Symphony might be called his *Werther*. There a heart-rending experience finds artistic release. I do not mean that he expresses in tone something he has lived—that would be programme music; what happens is that a mood born of recollection and of present feeling produces themes and affects the whole shape of the musical development without breaking the musical context. Thus a self-contained composition becomes a personal message from his heart. I am not going to examine the symphony in detail; no need to dwell on the youthful fire of the first movement or the powerful scherzo, with its enchanting trio. Anything of the kind would detract from their rich musical content. The third movement, however, sounded something new in music, and its significance justifies examination. A spiritual reaction to a tragic event is translated into music in the 'Funeral March in the Manner of Callot' and in the finale; there, the young composer frees himself from personal experience. The very vehemence of Mahler's emotion may well have made him unaware of his own audacity in using the spectral creeping of the canon, with its tones of brazen scorn and shrill laughter, as the musical medium for dull, lowering despair; but the imagination, novelty, and relentless veracity of the work bear the imprint of genius. It is not surprising that the audience was dumbfounded at the first performance. Then, in the fourth movement, all his passionate vehemence breaks out, and with unrelenting force, wins a victory over life.

Some time in December 1909—the last year but one of his life—Mahler wrote to me from America after a performance of the First: 'I was pretty well satisfied with this youthful tryout. I have a queer experience when I conduct any of these works. A burningly painful sensation crystallizes. What a world is mirrored in these sounds and figures! The Funeral March and the storm that follows are a flaming indictment of the Creator!' After years during which he had not heard it, this elementally expressive music could still shake its composer. In its emotional excess, its unconditional and unconscious audacity of new expression, its wealth of invention, the symphony has the unique impact of the youthful work of genius. Proliferating in invention and pulsing with passion, it is music that has been lived.

From then on, the composer turned aside from personal experiences. The natural bent of his mind shifted his gaze to the tragic existence of man. He conceived the elegiac vision of the opening movement of his Second Symphony—the mourning chant of a suffering world. It starts and every hearer feels: thus begins a symphony! With irresistible force and Beethovian majesty it takes hold of us; the sense of controlled tragedy finds concentrated expression. The gloomy theme is wrought into a movement powerful in invention, development, contrast, architecture; a master has found his style. Here is the sonata form—exposition, development, recapitulation, coda. No one regarding this lofty structure, brilliant in light and shade, with drastic contradictions and fateful contractions of musical polyphony, can accept the laconic description—'a funeral service'—which was all that Mahler could indicate when asked what he 'had in mind'. It seems incredible for anyone to speak of programme music, looking from that concept to this music, but there were some who did so at the time.

The music of the First, especially in its third and fourth movements, is still tinged with and influenced by personal experience. In the Second the world of thought and feeling is farther away from the music. That world, in the first three movements, is a mere background of moods without any continuity of thought, without constant influence of emotions on the music, which lives its own life: it has dissolved mood, feeling, thought, into itself and transformed them into music. The second movement, a charming, delightful andante, is even more absolutely musical than the first; Mahler, in conversation, used to call it a happy episode in the life of the hero, whose obsequies occupy the first movement. The third derives from a sinister mood; it is as though suddenly the wild chaos of existence were seen as unreal, ghostly. Perhaps the most original of the scherzos, this one is full of fantastic life; a scurrilous humour and wild flashes of light play over its sinister, dank-flowing surface, to emerge in a lamenting 'Call of the Wild', with no definite idea or thought behind it. It has become a masterpiece of symphonic music.

At this point, I want to interrupt the course of my survey to indicate that while a composer can translate moods, ideas, and feelings into music, music, in its turn, calls forth ideas. In his *Birth of Tragedy from the Spirit of Music* Nietzsche says that music scatters pictures like sparks, though its nature is such that its pictures are different in kind from those which may have sponsored them. In the creative process there is often a loosely woven interplay between music and idea. Dreamlike images rise and fade, give stimulus, feeling, and colour to the music; they alternate with periods of thought and indistinct moods, while music follows its own path, obeys the law of its own logic. An example of the unconnected dreamlike unreality of the world in which music floats is given by Mahler's story of how, at the bold conclusion of the first movement of the First, he saw Beethoven before him, breaking out into peals of laughter and running off. The laughing Beethoven has really nothing to do with the experiences out of which, by Mahler's own account, the First Symphony arose. It is indeed so unprogrammatic as to constitute in itself a *reductio ad absurdum* more effective than any aesthetic argument of the view that Mahler wrote programme music. Again, apropos of the eerie atmosphere of the scherzo in the Second, Mahler said that it was as ghostly as the distant sight of couples dancing to unheard music—a picture that makes it impossible to see the Second as an unfolding of programme music.

In the fourth movement—to return to my thesis —words are sung: with the *Urlicht*, they light up the impenetrable flood of tone, woven of moods, but shaped in accordance with its own laws. Man sings —in pious words taken from *Des Knaben Wunderhorn* —of his confident trust that God will give him a candle to lead him to the life of eternal bliss. Here we are—nearly—given a programme for the next movement: wandering in the shine of the *Urlicht*. Some such vision did determine the general form of the movement; idea and music draw close: Mahler's imagination is dominated by the Last Judgment, and from the opening of the fifth movement on, one can sense a conflict between a succession of mental images and the course of the music. Music has to give way, and that is easy to understand when one recalls the emotions of a man possessed by such ideas. Yet, with the marchlike development of the choral themes, the musician is again in command; he hands over to the poet only with the entry of the *Grosser*

Appell. With the sublime music into which Mahler transformed Klopstock's poem on the Resurrection —and to which he added in verse the expression of his hopes and convictions—he answers for the first time the sorrow, the doubt, the questions that wrung his soul. In transfigured sounds, inspired by the lofty message of his heart, he reaches the solemn assurance of the close: 'I shall die, to live!' 'Rise, yea, my heart, thou shalt rise after brief rest, and what thou hast endured shall carry thee to God!'

Now he can look out hopefully, with an enhanced sense of life. 'How fair the meadows seem today,' says Parsifal, looking in reverence on the face of nature. Such was Mahler's mood; as he gazed on nature with love and deep emotion, he felt it within himself, felt its heartbeat in his own heart. In his Third Symphony nature itself seems to be transformed into sound. In it alone the movements follow a determined sequence of idea. The original headings to the movements were *Pan erwacht: der Sommer marschiert ein* (Pan awakes; summer marches in); *Was mir die Blumen auf der Wiese erzählen* (What the flowers in the meadow tell me); *Was mir die Tiere im Walde erzählen* (What the animals in the wood tell me); *Was mir die Nacht erzählt* (What the night tells me); *Was mir die Morgenglocken erzählen* (What the morning bells tell me); and *Was mir die Liebe erzählt* (What love tells me). The night now speaks of man, the morning bells speak of angels, and love speaks of God—we can see the basic structural unity of the symphony. For this very reason; he could do without the titles, which were dropped like a scaffolding when the house is ready; he wanted to have the work taken as pure music. He was right; it had become music.

But there is one exception: with the trumpet calls, drum rolls, drastic vulgarities, and fiery march-rhythms of the first movement, with its majestic trombone solo and humming trills on the muted strings, an abundance of strange events and thoughts seem to be rather musically described than composed. They are only insufficiently explained by the title—*Pan erwacht: der Sommer marschiert ein*. Some of the subsidiary titles are yet stranger. On one—*Was mir das Felsgebirg erzählt*—I have already touched; others are—*Das Gesindel* (The Mob), where, in the development section, cellos and basses open a grotesque episode; and *Sudstürm* (Southern Storm), with wild string passages near its close. Indeed, when one assembles all these headings and ideas one perceives with astonishment that there is, in fact, no internal connection, and that, in many cases, the music has evoked the picture rather than the picture the music. What, one asks, is the real content of the movement? What is it about? Two opposing, panic-filled basic moods—primordial inflexibility and lust-driven wildness—have been transformed into a wealth of musical images. Out of them Mahler builds a movement extraordinary in architecture and not less so in content. In the ecstasy of composition, new images, new thoughts were thrown in from moment to moment; unconnected as they are, they

might produce confusion rather than clarity, and are
not at all suited to be formed into a 'programme'. In
regard to this movement—and to this one alone—
I must admit that the effort to take it in musically is
frequently thwarted by the intrusion of non-musical
matter, of fantastic images, that break the musical
texture. And yet, I feel that here, for once, the wild
unconcerned genius should compensate us for the
problematic style. In this movement Mahler decided
to dispense with titles confident that the unique
creation of a wide-ranging imagination would be
accepted as the voice of nature, all the more as
aesthetic lines are likely to be blurred when humour
—under the sign of which the work exists—flickers
brightly.

Beginning with the second movement, it becomes
different. Here a delightful theme is developed
purely musically; even if tinged by the 'flower
mood', it is designed as music and requires no
thought of flowers to be understood. No resemblance
here, to the 'Witches' Sabbath' of Berlioz's *Symphonie fantastique*, in which one must cling to the
image of the wild spook to comprehend the musical
content of the score. The third movement is, like
the second, genuinely symphonic. A dream of the
universe took possession of Mahler's mind, and his
soul lovingly poured itself out in music. But as the
dream passed from flowers and animals to mankind,
he longed for the word, and moved by the mystery
of human destiny changing between grief and joy, he
made Nietzsche's *Mitternachtsgedicht* the poetic theme

for the nocturnal music of the fourth movement. In
the fifth movement, again he wanted words for the
joyful tidings of the Angels. Certain lines in *Des
Knaben Wunderhorn* had always moved him and lifted
his spirit:

> Hast thou broken the ten commands?
> Down on thy knees and pray to God!
> Pray to God every day,
> And heavenly joy shall come thy way.

From this angelic message, he worked out a solemn
music, with clear-toned bells ringing, happy boys
and women singing in chorus, and sinful humanity
receiving the blessed tidings. In the final movement,
words are stilled; what language can utter heavenly
love with more power, more force, than pure
music? The adagio, with its broad, solemn melo-
dious line, is, as a whole, and despite passages of
burning pain, eloquent of comfort and grace: it is a
single sound of heartfelt and exalted feelings in which
the whole giant structure finds its musical culmina-
tion. Mahler called the Third his 'joyful wisdom'.
Essentially it communicates a joyous outlook on life
and the universe.

This mood rises in the Fourth to a singularly
exalted gladness. In the Second he had sung: 'On
wings I soar, for which I have fought': he might,
although in a more fantastic vein, have said the same
of the Third. And now he was borne upward as in a
dream: the earth was no longer under his feet. The
music of the Fourth tells of this floating sensation;

the themes of its final movement connect with the angelic movement of the Third and also, on the whole, continue its inner mood. After his solemn works he felt a longing for gladness, or rather for serenity. The outcome was the idyllic Fourth, in which inward piety dreams a dream of Heaven. The whole atmosphere, indeed, is dreamlike and unreal; the solemnity often audible in the Third is hidden here behind a mysterious smile and whimsical humour. The Fourth is a fairy tale; the power and pathos of its predecessors are translated into airy imponderability; the thundering vision proclaimed by a prophet is now confirmed by an angel's gentle voice. Earth has been left behind and a blissful exaltation colours the music. Here, however, the situation differs from that of the Third: it comes from afar. The three orchestral movements proceed without carrying over the highly individual mood of their origin into more definite images. Even the *Kleiner Appell* of the first movement does not lead to any larger poetic vision. There is a hint of droll humour in the first movement and in the *Himmlisches Leben* (Heavenly Life), which strangely harmonizes with the loftiness of tone pervading the work. The scherzo is a kind of uncanny fairy tale; its demoniac solo for violin, like the charming trio, is in marked contrast to the rest of the work, and yet retains its lightness and its mystery. Of the andante, with its restful depth and lucid beauty, Mahler told me that when he wrote it he had a vision of a tombstone on which was carved an image

of the departed, with folded arms, in eternal sleep.
The words of the poem in the last movement depict
the atmosphere that gave rise to the Fourth; its
picture of childlike joys symbolizes heavenly bliss,
and at the close music is hailed as the supreme joy;
the humorous tone passes gently over into one of
exalted solemnity.

Mahler's first four symphonies reveal a significant
part of his inner history. In them the power of the
musical language responds to the force of the spiritual
experience. They also have in common a continuous
interchange between the world of sound and the
world of ideas, thoughts, and feelings. In the First
the music reflects the stormy emotions of a subjective
experience; beginning with the Second metaphysical
questions demand answers and solutions. The reply
is threefold and is given from a fresh standpoint each
time. The Second is concerned with the meaning of
the tragedy of human life: the clear reply is its justification by immortality. Assuaged, he turns, in the
Third, to nature, and after traversing its cycle,
reaches the happy conviction that the answer is in
'omnipotent love, all-forming, all-embracing'. In the
Fourth he assures himself and us through a lofty and
cheerful dream of the joys of eternal life, that we
are safe.

Now the struggle to achieve a new vision of the
universe in terms of music is suspended. Now full of
strength and equal to life's demands, he is ready to
write music as a musician. His Fifth Symphony is a
work full of power and sane self-confidence which

turns its face towards life and reality. Its movements are a powerful funeral march leading into the agitated first movement; a scherzo of imposing scale; an adagietto, and a rondo-fugue. Nothing in my talks with Mahler, not a single note in the work, suggests that any extrinsic thought or emotion entered into its composition. Here is music. Passionate, wild, heroic, exuberant, fiery, solemn, tender, it covers the whole gamut of feeling. But it is 'merely' music. And not even from afar do metaphysical questions cross its purely musical course. But the musician in him tried all the more eagerly to develop his symphonic craft, even to create new and higher forms. The Fifth demanded, in its heightened polyphony, a renewing of his style of orchestration. Here begins a new phase of his development, and we now have in the Fifth a masterpiece that shows its composer at the zenith of his life, his powers, and his craft. There is a certain sense in which the Fifth, Sixth, and Seventh belong together. Both of the latter are as unmetaphysical as music can be, in them the composer is concerned to expand the symphonic idea. However, the Sixth is bleakly pessimistic: it reeks of the bitter taste of the cup of life. In contrast with the Fifth, it says 'No', above all in its last movement, where something resembling the inexorable strife of 'all against all' is translated into music. 'Existence is a burden; death is desirable and life hateful', might be its motto. Mahler called it his 'Tragic'. The mounting tension and climaxes of the last movement resemble, in their grim power, the mountainous waves of a sea that will overwhelm and destroy the ship; the work ends in hopelessness and the night of the soul. '*Non placet*' is his verdict on this world; the 'other world' is not glimpsed for a moment.

The Seventh likewise falls into the absolutely musical, purely symphonic, group. These three works needed no words to clarify their conceptual ideas, and consequently no voices are used. For this reason, I cannot discuss them. I could never talk about the music itself, and there is no need to analyse it; analysis on these lines has long been available. Note, however, the reappearance of the seemingly long-buried Romantic, significant and humanly illuminating, in the three central movements of the Seventh. These three nocturnal pieces, steeped in the emotions of the past, reveal that the master of the superb first movement and of the brilliant rondo is again involved in that longing for fulfilment, that search for answers to his questions about life, which always haunted him.

At this crucial juncture, he came upon the Hymn of Hrabanus Maurus and turned all his highly developed symphonic powers to giving an answer to the most heart-searching of all questions, by placing in a full-scale musical context the *Veni, Creator Spiritus* and the belief in immortality voiced by Goethe in the final scene of *Faust*. This was his Eighth Symphony. No other work expresses so fully the impassioned 'Yes' to life. 'Yes' resounds here in the massed voices of the hymn wrought by a master hand into the temple-like structure of a symphonic movement; it peals from the *Faust* words and from the torrent of music in which Mahler's own emotion is released. Here, advanced in years, the seeker after God confirms, from a higher plane, the assurance which his youthful heart had poured out in the passion of the Second Symphony. In the later work the relation between idea and music is absolutely clear: from the first, the word is integral; from the first, eternity is the issue of which the symphony is born, to which it is the reply.

Can the man who reared the structure of the Eighth 'in harmony with the Everlasting', be the same as the author of the *Trinklied vom Jammer der Erde* (Drinking Song of Earthly Woe) —the man who slinks alone, in autumn, to the trusty place of death in search of comfort, who looks at youth with the commiserating eyes of age, at beauty with muted emotion, who seeks to forget in drink the senselessness of life and finally leaves it in deep melancholy? Is it the same master who, after his gigantic symphonies, constructs a new form of unity out of six songs? He is scarcely the same as a man or as a composer. All his previous work had grown out of his sense of life. Now the knowledge that he had serious heart trouble was, as with the wounded Prince Andrei in Tolstoi's *War and Peace*, breaking his inner hold on life. The loosening of all previous ties altered his entire outlook. *Das Lied von der Erde* is, in terms of the sentence of Spinoza already quoted, written *sub specie mortis*. Earth is vanishing; he breathes in another air, a new light shines on him — and so it is a wholly new work that Mahler wrote:

new in its style of composition, new in invention, in instrumentation, and in the structures of the various movements. It is more subjective than any of his previous works, more even than his First. There, it was the natural 'I' of a passionate youth whose personal experience obstructed his view of the world; here, while the world slowly sinks away, the 'I' becomes the experience itself—a limitless range of feeling opens for him who soon will leave this earth. Every note carries his individual voice; every word, though based on a poem a thousand years old, is his own, *Das Lied von der Erde* is Mahler's most personal utterance, perhaps the most personal utterance in music. His invention, which from the Sixth on had been significant less in itself than as material for his formative hand, here achieves a highly personal stamp. In this sense, it is accurate to call *Das Lied* the most Mahlerian of his works.

'*Der Abschied*' (Farewell), title of the last song in *Das Lied*, might serve as rubric for the Ninth Symphony. Its first movement is derived from the mood of *Das Lied*, though in no sense musically related to it. It develops from its own thematic material into the kind of symphonic form which he alone could now create. It is a noble paraphrase of the *Abschied*, shattering in its tragedy. The movement floats in an atmosphere of transfiguration achieved by a singular transition between the sorrow of farewell and the vision of the radiance of Heaven—an atmosphere derived not from imagination, but from immediate feeling. Its invention is as Mahlerian as that of *Das*

Lied. The second movement, the old, familiar scherzo in a new form—this time the main tempo is broad—reveals a wealth of variations, with a tragic undertone sounding through the happiness: 'The dance is over.' The defiant *agitato* of the third movement shows once more Mahler's stupendous contrapuntal mastery; the last voices a peaceful farewell; with the conclusion, the clouds dissolve in the blue of Heaven. In design, movement, technique, and polyphony, the Ninth continues the line of the Fifth, Sixth, and Seventh symphonies. It is, however, inspired by an intense spiritual agitation: the sense of departure. And although it is also purely orchestral music, it differs from the middle group, is nearer to the earlier symphonies in its deeply subjective emotional mood.

In our art the new, challenging, revolutionary, passes, in the course of time, over into the known, accepted, familiar. The lasting validity of Faust's great idea is not owing to the fact that he wrested new territory from the encroaching sea; only when the new becomes the old do thoughts and actions reveal their importance. Mahler, an adventurer of the mind, left behind him in music a certain stretch of newly conquered territory, but as the decades pass, his works should no longer be expected to sound sensational. Yet, strangely enough, they still generate excitement; Mahler's feeling and unrestricted drive for self-revelation were far too elemental in his music for it to become cosily familiar and be taken for granted. The daring spirit flames high whenever the notes are heard. But should not the interpreter be distrusted whose performance of the works of Bach, Beethoven, or Wagner conveys an impression of easy possession? Have we not learned from Mahler's conducting that it is possible to make such works always sound as if they were being performed for the first time? Adequate performances of Mahler's own works today will surely reveal a Titan. Anything new in music and the drama needs the protection of congenial interpretation.

There is, however, a gradual fading of the sound, and as time passes, the daring is bound to pale, to lose its edge, especially in lesser interpretations. This raises the question of how much daring and adventurousness really signify in a work of art. Mere daring, aimed at challenge and novelty, is certain to wear off; only together with profound and permanent values is it assured of lasting effect. If the works of these Promethean masters are rewarded with immortality, the reason lies in their creative power, depth of feeling, and, above all, beauty. For beauty is immortal; it can preserve the mortal charm of the merely 'interesting' from decay.

So the supreme value of Mahler's work lies not in the novelty of its being intriguing, daring, adventurous, or bizarre, but rather in the fact that this novelty was transfused into music that is beautiful, inspired, and profound; that it possesses the lasting values of high creative artistry and a deeply significant humanity. These keep it alive today, these guarantee its future.

IV

THE PERSONALITY

EVERYONE who knew Mahler will recall how often his expression would change suddenly from cheerfulness to gloom. It was as though he was reproaching himself for having lightly forgotten some sorrow. The root of these fits of depression, which, though they never ceased, were less frequent in his later years, I did not, at first, discern; then I came to realize that a profound sense of the misery of this world would rise in icy waves from the centre of his being and overwhelm his spirit. 'What grim darkness underlies life,' he said to me once, deeply affected, and his distracted countenance still marked by the spiritual paroxysms from which he had emerged. He went on to speak in broken accents of the tragic dilemma of human existence. 'Whence have we come? Whither are we bound? Is it true, as Schopenhauer says, that I willed this life before I was conceived? Why do I fancy I am free, when my character constricts me like a prison? To what purpose is all this toil and suffering? How can cruelty and evil be the handiwork of a loving God? Will death at last reveal the meaning of life?' Lamentation, astonishment, horror would pour out, in a torrent of words like these, as though a geyser had been turned on. He never really found deliverance in his agonized effort to find sense in human life. He was distracted by ardent activity: he was helped by his sense of humour to cast off the burden; a vivid concern about intellectual questions strengthened him and helped to still a nearly unquenchable thirst for knowledge and comprehension. Yet his spirit never knew escape from the torturing question —For What? It was the driving impulse of his creative activity. Each work was a fresh effort to find the answer, and even when he found it, the old, unassuageable longing would rise anew. His nature was such that he could not hold any achieved spiritual position; none had constancy. Impulse ruled his life and work, and so each spiritual gain had to be won afresh. This meant that everything—life, art, personal relationships—was new each day; it also meant that he was denied the blessings of a sense of systematic advance or the mastery and evaluation of experience. Each day with him saw the struggle and the sacrifice renewed. He could not have been taken as a model for the hero of a *Bildungsroman*; steady development and what Goethe calls a reasoned use of experience, thought, and achievement were denied him, were not in his nature. At heart he was a romantic, and a romantic governed by the favourable—or unfavourable—aspects of the hour.

At the same time, it would be entirely false to describe him as vacillating or unstable. Constancy was not in him; yet his course was defined and unalterable by any impulse. Nor would it be true to call him unhappy. Categories like happy and unhappy do not fit a man so richly endowed, so warm of heart, so eloquent of tongue. He knew the passionate uplift of spirit as well as deep sorrow. Such a gamut of feeling is a greater gift of the gods than happiness. In sorrow, his faithful companion on life's path, he knew the consolation of which Tasso speaks: 'And, if man agonizes in silence, a God gave me the gift to speak my sorrow.' He spoke it in a tongue of which he had supreme command: his sufferings and longings became music. Constantly born anew, they were constantly translated into works of art.

But Mahler knew and spoke not only of ecstasies of longing, of distress, of spiritual devotion. He was both ready and willing to 'get outside himself', and richly endowed for communication on more serene levels. His soul's barometer was not set only to 'stormy' and 'changeable'. Frost, storms, heat waves did occur; so did gentler skies, and the warmth and joy of sunshine. This is evident in many works, for example, the serene andante of the Second Symphony and the *Rheinlegendchen*, which he called a piece of captured sunshine. Smiles and sudden gay laughter suited his features as well as his nature, though the shadow always hovered near.

I have touched on the 'nocturnal' element in his work. It was paralleled in his personality. It was the source of the very strong impression of something

demoniac in him which made him interesting to
everybody and terrifying to many. It remains one of
Nature's mysteries that it is able to create a consti-
tutionally sound human being combining such contradictions; a man who could be at one and the
same time endowed with so much energy, brilliance
of intellect, serenity, such dark vehemence, such
whimsical humour, and continually be menaced by
the dangerous depths within himself.

Because no spiritual experience, however hardly
won, was ever his secure possession, I cannot,
despite the religious cast of his mind, and its intermittent flights, call him a believer. Emotional excitement would carry him to transports of faith, but its
serene assurance was not within his scope. The
suffering of a creature touched too deeply; murder
in the animal kingdom, the cruelty of man to man,
the infirmities of the human frame, the continuous
menace of fate—all this again and again shook the
foundations of his belief. More insistent was the
problem of reconciling the suffering and evil of the
world with the goodness and omnipotence of God.
If his music expresses, as it does, his longing and his
questions, that music in its turn kept longing and
questioning alive, and forever rekindled them.
Music has, of course, an incomparable power of
drawing us towards the spiritual. In the phrase of
Nietzsche which I have already quoted, it scatters
images like sparks; it also sows the seeds of faith.
In its highest manifestations, it is mysteriously related to religion. The divine service needs music to

give the most solemn expression to piety. Music
lends compulsive power to the feeling of devotion
in ecclesiastical texts and to the religious scenes in
biblical oratorios. Independently of all this, absolute
music—for example, the andantes of Mozart or
Beethoven—produces, in its own right, an elevation
and lift of spirit otherwise accessible only through
religion.

This is not the place for a discussion of the relation
between religion and music. I merely note their
frequent association in visual art and how naturally
music appears in the works of Bellini and kindred
painters. Here the Giorgione 'Concerto' comes
again to mind. Not angels, to be sure, are making
here the lovely music, filled with a happy sense of
the goodness of God, which sounds in Mozart's or
Schubert's melodies; here it is not the elderly,
quiet viola da gamba player of the picture who is the
musician, but rather the pious monk, whose soul
burns with ascetic fervour. Here is a human eye that
seems longingly to search the heavenly distances:
here are fingers that might produce tones like
Beethoven's. Mahler's nature was of this order: he
looks out from the earth, whose suffering is his, and
seeks God. I stress the fact that his religious attitude
is throughout rooted in the relationship between
religion and music. Some musicians—and listeners to
music—are unaware of its transcendental power;
while steeped in music and genuinely musical, they
are devoid of any kind of religious sentiment, or even
awareness. Those, on the other hand, who strive to

penetrate beyond the earthly veil find in music a
support to and confirmation of faith.

Mahler's thoughts and aspirations strove towards
that 'other' world. Yet Goethe's phrase—'To the
efficient man the world is not mute'—applies to
him. Faustian as he was, and forever compelled to
seek the ultimate meaning of everything that is,
everything that happens, he was, at the same time,
bound by a multiplicity of ties and interests to this
earthly sphere and to the spiritual life within it. He
was passionately interested in advances in the natural
sciences. A physicist friend who kept him in detailed
touch with the progress of research spoke elo-
quently of the keen and thorough understanding
shown by his questions. His favourite reading was
the philosophical aspects of science; Lotze's *Micro-
cosmos* occupied him for a long time, especially in its
development of the theory of the atom. A lasting
impression was made by Fechner's *Zend-Avesta*, and
he delighted in *Nana, or the Spiritual Life of Plants* by
the same author. Needless to say, he was throughout
his life deeply influenced by Goethe's general attitude to Nature and his prolific work in this field.
But he was never merely on the receiving end. His
own productive intelligence was constantly at work
on problems arising out of his reading and contacts.
I remember an occasion when he tried to interpret
the law of gravitation as repulsion by the sun, and in
conversation with a well-known physicist tried in
his impassioned way to convince the latter by
adducing other related cosmic ideas. Again, some-

body said in his presence that when an earthworm was cut in two, two new units were produced, the back part growing a new head and thus an independent existence: 'That,' he cried, 'is proof against Aristotle's doctrine of entelechy.' He was far too sensible and far too well aware of the gaps in his scientific equipment to be dogmatic, but his lively interest in questions of the kind was not satisfied by the mere acquisition of knowledge. The vitality of his mind compelled him to wrestle with problems on his own, and he was delighted when, after meeting and overcoming instructed contradiction, he felt that he had touched a deeper level of understanding. In discussion the intuitive quality of his remarks invariably called forth the admiration of scientific friends.

When I first knew him, in Hamburg, he was completely under the influence of Schopenhauer. Nietzsche made a powerful but not a lasting impression. He was attracted by the poetic fire of *Zarathustra*, but repelled by the core of its intellectual content. Nietzsche's anti-Wagnerism made him indignant, and later he turned against him; the aphorist was bound to antagonize the master of symphonic form. In his later years he was taken by the philosophy of Hartmann. But the sun in the sky of his spiritual world was Goethe. He had a remarkable knowledge of his work, and, thanks to a unique memory, would quote endlessly from it. He was a constant reader of Goethe's conversations with Eckermann and others, and Goethe's discussion of immortality with

Falk was one of the foundations of his intellectual life.

Among German poets, Hölderlin was nearest to him; poems like 'Patmos' and 'Der Rhein' were sacred possessions constantly at hand. With deep feeling he often quoted to me from the splendid, enigmatic lines written by Hölderlin after his mental disturbance. Among the mystics he preferred Angelus Silesius; with him he felt a close relationship, deriving comfort from such bold and exalted sense of nearness to God. His giving the name 'Titan' to his First Symphony signalized his love of Jean-Paul; we often talked about this great novel, and especially about the character of Roquairol, whose influence is noticeable in the Funeral March. Mahler would insist that an element of Roquairol, of his self-centred, self-tormenting, scornful and imperilled spirit, exists in every gifted individual, and has to be conquered before productive powers can come into play. He felt entirely at home with the witty and complex humour of Schoppe. *Siebenkäs* was a favourite work, and, he insisted, Jean-Paul's masterpiece. In his younger days his heart was naturally given to E. T. A. Hoffmann, who attracted him by his glowing imagination, force, and humour, and especially by his 'nocturnal' quality. Sterne's *Tristram Shandy* was among his favourites, also because of its humour. He often remarked that, but for the antidote of humour, the tragedy of human existence would have been unendurable. In the course of conversation he loved to refer to episodes like the opening of the will in Jean-Paul's *Flegeljahre*, or to recall details of Dostoevski's *A Silly Affair*, each time laughing happily and loudly. His own sense of humour abounded in droll fancies, and his wit had a sharp edge. He also appreciated pointed remarks by others, if they were made spontaneously, and was often delighted by the most harmless witticism. On the other hand, he disapproved of telling 'funny' anecdotes or jokes: his face would go stony and for a while he would be out of temper as though pained by seeing fine fruits of fancy preserved in a tin. He loathed coarseness, and I cannot recall any remark of the kind made in his presence, far less by him. This aversion did not, of course, apply to the coarseness of a given period, as found in Shakespeare, Cervantes, Sterne, and others; then he took it as part and parcel of a work of art. A compelling affinity of mind bound him to the work of Dostoevski, who profoundly influenced his whole outlook. Indeed, what I have called his sense of the woe of the world is fully expressed in the conversation between Ivan and Alyosha in *The Brothers Karamazov*.

I have cited but a few examples of Mahler's endlessly diversified, comprehensive interest in things of the mind. Pictorial art came comparatively late into his life, and artist as he was in revealing the passion, the 'nocturnal' in the realm of sound, the visual aspect never meant much to him. The one painter who deeply moved him was Rembrandt, a kindred spirit. Visual art was never a necessity of his life in the sense in which poetry and literature, science and philosophy, were indispensable to him.

It would be a mistake to see in the variety of Mahler's interests the mere dilettantism of a restless mind. The criterion of dilettantism is accumulation of knowledge without its assimilation. Mahler had a sure, selective instinct for the intellectual food that would strengthen him for the mission of his life. He was driven by the law of his nature to seek the ultimate meaning of the events, the actions, the pains of existence; his study was consciously directed towards equipping him for this task. In his exploration of the spiritual world the needle of his compass pointed imperturbably in one direction: upwards. His learning thus became experience and was assimilated into his being; it had a steady metaphysical aim. His many-sidedness was of the surface; one would be nearer the truth if one spoke of the superb unity of a mind that brought an equal spiritual intensity to musical composition and to intellectual studies, and directed both by the light of a single aim.

True, there was no conscious system or method in his self-education; here again impulse was guide. While there is something magnificent in his conquest of the treasures of the mind, it failed to give him the definite outlook that might have stilled his restless heart. His style of life was set, the direction decided; but moved by impulse rather than by planned continuity.

Mahler's conversation was a perfect mirror of the multifariousness of his intellectual interests. It showed

a man deeply absorbed in cosmic problems, poig-
nantly aware of the sorrows of humanity, who pur-
sued knowledge along every available path and
sought release in creative work from the struggle
within himself. The wealth and versatility of his
intellect, his warmth of feeling and firmness of
judgment, were matched by his inexhaustible choice
of topics, the liveliness and sureness of his talk.
Moreover, he never committed the common fault
of not attending to his companion: he could listen
as well as talk. And he was able and ready to give all
of himself completely—a rare virtue. He never used
his sagacity just to score easy dialectical victories—
he was interested only in pertinent discussion of the
matter at hand. Of course he loved a good argument
and had unusual skill in putting his point of view in
swift and telling terms. He also appreciated good,
homely, leisurely talks, and liked to listen to lively
and coherent recounting of tales—he himself was as
interesting as a storyteller as he was stimulating as a
listener.

I remember many a conversation that began in the
afternoon in a *Kaffeehaus*, was carried on during long
walks, and continued with unabated liveliness all
through our supper. Then when it was time to say
good-bye, he would say that we had solved the
seven problems of the universe, and so everything
was settled.

His talent and taste for improvisation, so marked
a feature of his interpretative work, lent the charm
of endless surprise to his talk. Once as he was walk-

ing by the side of a mountain stream, a musician in his company sighed that musical possibilities were now exhausted; after Beethoven, Wagner, Bruckner, and so on, there was nothing left to be done. Mahler stopped in his tracks, and pointing to the water, exclaimed in tones of surprise: 'Look, my dear friend!' 'What at?' 'The last wave!' This I had at second hand, but I remember his saying in reply to a remark that a certain new composition was interesting: 'Interesting is easy, beautiful is difficult.' His quickness of uptake, like his turn for the barbed phrase, sometimes produced remarks that were more puzzling than convincing, but he yielded to temptation only occasionally, and he soon returned to serious analysis of the topic under discussion. It was the particular charm of his conversation that, whatever the subject, it *was* conversation; even where the theme was serious or heavy, he would import something easy, enjoyable, unbuttoned. Then he was at his most lovable; his talk, however light, never degenerated into chat or, however serious, into a lecture.

Mahler's morals have been the subject of much misunderstanding. People who admired the artist often censored his character. To dispel misapprehensions of this kind it is only necessary to read his letters, and I urge anyone who wants to understand him to read them. In them the warmth of his heart, his attachment to his friends, and his outgoing sympathy speak with beautiful distinctness. Misconceptions were no doubt owing largely to the fact that, while fully able to share in the joys and sorrows of others and eager to help them, he was likely to regard the world with the absent-minded glance of the creative artist. A man whose immense gifts are concentrated on creative work cannot conduct his life on a plan of well-regulated ethical activity. When he realized a case of need he was always ready to help, and to make sacrifices in order to do so. He was full of affection—his music shows that. Yet, like many a creative spirit, he was likely to forget man while loving humanity. When he did see him, he was endlessly kind, but for the most part, his gaze was turned inwards. I used to call his relation to his friends one of 'intermittent loyalty'. He could let long stretches of time go by in complete separation from them, physical and mental; the vacuum passed, he would be as warm and sympathetic as before.

Of petty faults he had none. Money had no meaning for him. To earning or saving he gave no thought until, at forty-seven, he left Vienna with the future weighing heavy on his mind. His 'ungrateful' programmes show how little he was affected by the occupational diseases of vanity and desire for success. When he was invited to give a series of concerts in St. Petersburg, I voiced a doubt about how the audience would react to his programmes. 'I never thought of that!' he exclaimed. When, in response to my pleadings, he drew up a fresh programme, he asked me: 'Is that applause-pushing enough?' This droll expression registered his contempt for ap-

plause. Wholly dedicated to the work itself, he was
without conceit; he found open praise unendurable.
This of course went with a sense of his own strength
and powers so secure that no opposition could shake
it. Belittlement of his achievement did not affect
him; he knew no envy of the success of others,
when deserved, though undeserved and unworthy
triumphs gave him a feeling of painful indignation.
The worship of false gods often brought to his lips
Schiller's words: 'I saw the sacred wreaths of fame
profaned by vulgar brows.'

I have to admit, have indeed already admitted,
that his outward demeanour left much to be desired,
from the conventional, social standpoint. Kindly at
heart, he could be harsh and biting, intransigent and
swift to anger, cold and forbidding; but he was
always sincere. Despite his commanding professional
position, this child of nature never learned—and
never wanted to learn—the unobliging obligingness,
the smoothness of polite society. A commanding
personality, he unconsciously demanded that others
should fit in with him—and most of them did.

So far, the outline I have attempted to draw of his
mind and spirit has been, so to say, vertical. It needs
to be made horizontal; to be related to the course
of time during which countless impressions have
gone to build up my present clear picture, a picture
often seen only in its general contour during the
seventeen years of my contact with the current of
his life under the changing climate of events. Save
for the reservation that must be made in any attempt

to reduce a living being to definition, the course of
Mahler's development seems to me to be divided
into three stages, which include within their temporal limits his creative work, his re-creative work,
and his personality.

The first stage presents the young man, searching,
suffering, uncontrolled; strong with the strength of
youth, finding his creative element in the world of
nature and folklore expressed in *Des Knaben Wunderhorn*. This takes him up to the termination of the
Fourth Symphony (1900); in the re-creative field,
it covers the first tumultuous years of his directorship of the Vienna Opera. The second stage shows
a man at the zenith of his powers, his gaze, to a
certain degree, on the 'here' and 'now', a conductor, carrying on a systematic battle with the
world for the realization of his artistic aims, and a
creator, influenced by Rückert and writing the symphonies from Five to Eight, inclusive. The third
stage shows a loosening hold on the day-to-day
world, a certain abnegation of the will to action, a
redirection of gaze farther into the distance. As conductor he was, except for his performances of his
Seventh and Eighth symphonies, withdrawn from my
sight, being in America, while as a creative artist,
stimulated by the Chinese lyrics, he was reaching
fulfilment with *Das Lied von der Erde* and his Ninth
Symphony.

The first stage was dominated by that central
theme—the longing for God of a man tormented
by the sorrows of the world—which I should call

the 'constant' element in his whole life. Closely related to this is his nearness to Nature. It provided an attitude akin to that of Faust when he says to the Deity: 'Thou gavest me no chill astonished visit, rather permitted me to gaze into the secrets of thy bosom, as a friend. . . . Thou hast taught me to know my brothers in the still woods, in the air, and in the waters.' But Mahler transcended this, his relation to Nature was more elemental. In 1896 he wrote to the editor of a musical periodical: 'It seems strange to me that most people, when speaking of "nature", have in mind only flowers, birds, the scent of the forest, etc. No one seems to know the great Dionysus, the God Pan.' He, of course, knew him well; the first, Pan-like, movement of the Third Symphony shows this. At the same time, no Dionysiac sense of Nature, nor any devotion to creatures, could make him a pantheist, as the last movement shows. Originally, he had called this movement 'What love tells me', and added the lines: 'Father, look upon my pain, and let no creature die in vain.' This is not a deification of Nature; still less is the adagio; it is personal religious confession.

Indeed, the great *moral* achievement of Mahler's life seems to me to lie in the fact that neither the torments of the creature nor the pangs of the human spirit caused him comfortably to shrug shoulders with the '*Ignorabimus*' of the philosopher, and turn away, withers unwrung, to look at what the world has to give of beauty and happiness. In his gloomier moments, the words spoken in Mickiewicz's poem

'Funeral Rites', 'Thou art not the Father of man-kind, but their Czar', might rise to his lips. But the spasm was brief. He recognized the misunderstanding implied. He was faithful to the task laid upon him: to extract a divine significance from his suffering.

The second stage shows a highly limited adjust-ment to this world by the child of nature and the seeker after God—this world, which, all said and done, constitutes the atmosphere, however prob-lematic, of art. Works of art, conceived in solitude, yet demand for their realization great institutions and their public. Ten years of unbounded devotion to such a great institution, of the mutual inter-actions and the contacts involved, could not but rub off some of the intransigence and strangeness of an 'original'. Enough of the queer and aloof was left to provide matter for daily astonishment to people. He would reply to friendly admonishment by say-ing: 'A man's wild oats are often the best thing he has!' Or when a well-meaning official told him not to bang his head against a wall, he retorted: 'Why not? It will make a hole in it one day.' And yet it is plain that in the ten years of his directorship of the Opera, if he was not assimilated, at least he became acclimatized.

What of the seeker after God, in this second, 'worldly' stage? The man who battled with the world and wrested its prizes had to pay it some attention. He held fast to that higher plane, it always gave him guidance, but it became overlaid by his worldly work. While it was still the source from

which the Fifth, Sixth, and Seventh symphonies
came, it seems less of a dominating influence on their
course.

Toward the end of this stage, the metaphysical
drive breaks through all barriers in a Faustian out-
burst; the Eighth was born, the 'bearer of joy', as
he called it. He hymns the *Creator Spiritus*; questioning and longing speak with renewed force, to be
released and satisfied in the Goethean declaration of
faith taken from the final scene of *Faust*. With this
exalted recapitulation of his life's central theme the
period of activity is over, and the third stage begins.
Once again his gaze is turned away from the world.
His heart is threatened; he has forebodings of death.
The seeker after God faces a supreme crisis. He said,
in a letter to me in July 1908: 'If I am to find my
way back to myself, I have got to accept the horrors
of loneliness. I speak in riddles, since you do not
know what has gone on and is going on within me.
It is, assuredly, no hypochondriac fear of death, as
you suppose. I have long known that I have got to
die. . . . Without trying to explain or describe
something for which there probably are no words,
I simply say that at a single fell stroke I have lost
any calm and peace of mind I ever achieved. I stand
vis-à-vis de rien, and now, at the end of my life,
have to begin to learn to walk and stand.'

How did he surmount the crisis? The Chinese
poems are at hand; he sings *Das Lied von der Erde*.
When he was nineteen he closed a letter to a friend
with the words: 'Oh, beloved Earth, when wilt

thou take the deserted one to thy bosom? Oh,
Eternal Mother, receive a lonely, restless heart!'
Now doomed to die, he ends his most individual
work with the words: 'The dear Earth blooms in
Spring. Everywhere and forever blue tinges the
horizons! Ever, forever! . . .' Loving greeting to the
Earth was part of the nature of the young man, as
of the ageing one; now, under the shadow of his
nearing end, it filled his whole soul. It also speaks
from the Ninth, composed still later. And so he sur-
mounted his last crisis in the spirit of the passage
from Faust's monologue where, contemplating release by drinking the phial, he says:

> Forth to the open ocean leads my way,
> Beneath my feet the flashing waters play,
> To new shores I am called by a new day.

The glance at the 'dear Earth' was now a back-
ward one; Earth at the leave-taking shows a face of
tender loveliness. The mystic meaning of the following passage from a letter written early in 1909 indi-
cates the state of mind of one who looks at life with
the hand of death already on his shoulder: 'There is
so much too much I could say about myself that I
cannot even try to begin. I have gone through so
much during the last year and a half (i.e., since
knowing of his heart condition) that I can scarcely
speak of it. How can I attempt to describe such an
overwhelming crisis? I see everything in such a new
light; I am so much in transformation that it would
not surprise me to find myself in a new body (like

Faust in the final scene). I am more avid for life than ever, and find "the habit of being alive" sweeter than ever. The days of my life just now are like the Sibylline Books. . . . What nonsense it is to let one's self be submerged by the brutal whirlpool of life; to be false, even for a moment, to one's self and what is above ourselves. But I write at random; next moment, when I leave this room, I shall be just as silly as all the rest. What is it within us that thinks? What is it that acts?'

And now a magnificent and highly revealing sentence follows: 'Strange—when I hear music—even when I am myself conducting it—I hear quite definite answers to all my questions, and am wholly clear and sure. Or, in reality, I seem to feel clearly that they are not questions at all.' Hence came the new *light* in which he saw everything. After all his thinking, longing, struggling, he found the real consolation of his pain in music; in music, which as I have already sought to indicate, is a way to God closely akin to that of religion.

When asked what he believed in, Mahler often said: 'I am a musician; that says everything.' If, as he suggests in the letter from which I have quoted, he sometimes repined—went 'soft'—what was this but a sign of the toll that the loftiest of men—and not least those of his impulsive nature—have to pay for the common liability to physical illness.

What was indeed tragic was that towards the end the acuteness of his feverish illness dimmed the exaltation of his spirit. Until then he had been sustained by the transcendental sense of redemption of *Das Lied* and the Ninth Symphony. And that the questioning spirit had lived on; that he still had wanted to learn, reminds one truly of Tolstoi's beautiful legend of the three pious old men, whom the bishop visits on their island. Hundreds of times they let him teach them the Lord's Prayer, but they could never remember the words. Then, after they had learned it at last, and long after the bishop's ship had left their island, he saw them one night walking the waves after him because, they said, they had forgotten it again. And he, deeply moved, said to them: 'You walked over the sea; what have you to learn?'

So it was with Mahler. He had and knew far more than what he asked, for in him was music, in him was love. Therefore, I believe the redeemed will have learned that his faithful seeking already contained the answer—and his longing will have been stilled.

C